Scrap Patchwork & Quilting

By Marti Michell

Meredith Press®
New York, New York

Dear Crafter:

This inviting collection of patchwork and appliqué scrap quilts is both nostalgic and new. Many of the patterns are classics, yet, reinterpreted in a personal selection of fabrics, seem completely contemporary. Each patchwork block and quilt will evoke special memories associated with the "scrap" fabrics used.

The term "scrap quilts" is widely used to describe a quilt made from many different fabrics. Marti Michell, a leading crafts author, fabric and pattern designer, and teacher, broadens the term to mean any fabric—whether left over from an earlier effort, or collected because of the color or intriguing pattern. Moreover, the care that goes into making these quilts is consistent with today's interest in ecology and recycling.

Scrap Patchwork & Quilting is the fifth title in the Meredith Press annual quilting series. We at Meredith Press strive to bring you high-quality craft books, written by well-known authors and offering a wide range of useful and attractive projects for every skill level. Each book includes full-page color photographs of the finished projects, detailed instructions rigorously checked to ensure accuracy, step-by-step diagrams, and full-size patterns.

We hope the projects in *Scrap Patchwork & Quilting* provide you many enjoyable hours creating your own patchwork and quilting masterpieces, and hope you'll look forward to other books from Meredith Press.

Sincerely yours,

Connie Schrader, Executive Editor

For Meredith® Press
President: Joseph J. Ward
Vice President and Editorial Director Meredith® Books:
  Elizabeth P. Rice
Assistant: Ruth Weadock
Executive Editor: Connie Schrader
Editorial Assistant: Carolyn Mitchell
Project Editor: Bob Oskam, Rapid Transcript
Design: Remo Cosentino, Bookgraphics
Production Manager: Bill Rose
Photo Styling: Marti Michell and Stacy Michell
Photography: Bread and Butter Studio, Atlanta, Georgia
Location Shots: At Storehouse, Norcross, Georgia
Illustrations: Ann Davis Nunemacher

ISBN: 0-696-02365-2
Library of Congress Catalog Card Number: 85-51795

Printed in the United States of America
10 9 8 7 6 5 4 3 2 1

Acknowledgments

It's wonderful to receive credit as author of this book, but it certainly wasn't accomplished alone. For starters, we are all indebted to the generations of quilters, mostly anonymous, who created so many wonderful scrap quilts, including those that are featured in this book. The inspiration of those quilts is an ideal starting point.

Three guest quilts are featured. Thank you to Bettina Havig, Nancy Granner, and Ellen Rosintoski for their creativity and co-operation. While the ideas and general fabric choices for the other newly made items are mine, much of the piecing and quilting was accomplished by my studio associates, Ann Cookston, Martha Dudley, and Camellia Pesto.

Narda Dudley, Sally Cutler, Jenny Lynn, and Pat Wilens all contributed greatly appreciated writing assistance. I have great admiration for and appreciation of Bob Oskam's ability to add clarity to my copy, control my punctuation, and maintain style consistencies. The beautifully executed illustrations of Ann Davis Nunemacher add immeasurably to the written word. The graphic design of the book by Remo Cosentino is crucial to your enjoyment.

Stacy Michell was creative, resourceful, and energetic as she assisted me in the photo styling. Steve Rucker makes our photography days both fun and effective. Special thanks to Storehouse, Inc. and to Don Guthrie, the Senior Store Manager of the Storehouse on Dawson Blvd., Norcross, Georgia, for allowing us to photograph almost one-fourth of our shots there.

Finally, thank you to everyone at Meredith Press for their confidence, support, and effort, which really made the book possible, and especially to Connie Schrader, who continued to keep calm while guiding everyone through the many details of this production.

Contents

Introduction

It started innocently, more than twenty years ago. I was still a dedicated dressmaker when I decided it would be cute to piece together the scraps from my daughter's most recent dresses and make her a patchwork prairie dress. Little did I know that was the start of a love affair with scrap quilts. A year or two later, I bought my first antique quilt—it was a scrap quilt. Without realizing it, every quilt I made or purchased was a multi-print quilt. Now I understand and am willing to admit that I am partial to—have always been partial to—scrap quilts. While I have expanded my horizons in the intervening years, I still have a special attachment to scrap quilts.

Because I feel that scrap quilts are lively and full of enthusiasm, we have worked hard to create a book reflecting the same enthusiasm. We've included lots of color photographs and illustrated the text with easily followed line drawings. You will get plenty of information if all you do is "read the pictures." I hope, however, that you will also read the words.

The first four chapters are general and should be read as a preface to making any of the quilts. Finishing information, common to most of the quilts, is in Chapter 11. In order to include as many quilts as possible, any steps that are repetitious are cross-referenced between quilts. We trust a little inconvenience is worth the extra quilts included.

Making quilts is, of course, the best way to understand the information. As you prepare to make a quilt, please read all directions and comments before you begin. Even if you aren't making lots of quilts, you may want to scan through all of the chapters, as some of the best techniques and tidbits are described in one or other project's how-to section.

Several of the quilts shown are from our antique collection, but more are newly made, and for every antique quilt shown, the same design is also interpreted in current fabrics.

The most important thing to remember is that there are no rights and wrongs in quiltmaking. If you decide to enter quilts in competition, you will need to concern yourself with what you think most judges want to see, but until then, you, the quiltmaker, are the one to satisfy.

My thoughts and personal preferences are a result of my accumulated experiences and are offered simply as ideas and possibilities. Hopefully, some of them will help you develop your own style and methods more quickly and easily.

What Are Scrap Quilts and Why Are They So Popular?

In the purest sense of the word, it would seem that a scrap quilt should be made from fabric that is left after cutting out a garment, or cut from less-worn sections of a used garment and recycled, or at the least, made from fabric that is left after cutting quilt pieces.

The term "scrap quilts" has come to be more widely interpreted as a quilt made from many different fabrics. That is the meaning intended in this book. I wish there were another commonly accepted and understood word with the same charm and nostalgia as "scrap." "Multi-fabric quilt" sounds very clinical. "A quilt made from the fabric collection of Marti Michell" is just too wordy and rather pretentious. Maybe we can turn "scrap" into an acronym, SCRAP. What about Seriously Collected Rags Appliquéd or Pieced? (The word "rags," of course, is intended as an endearing reference to fabric, and is often so used in the textile industry.) Selectively Combined, Rigorously Assorted Pieces would also be meaningful and quite appropriate. The Society for Creatively Recycling with Appliqué or Patchwork . . . Now, that's getting close.

I wish I could just get my editor to let us capitalize Scrap Quilts. It doesn't matter to me that English professors don't consider "scrap quilts" a proper name. It is the subject of this book and I felt it would be nice to give it that recognition, but no such persuasion. Far more important than the name, however, is the enjoyment.

From my reference point, scrap quilts are not just quilts made from leftover fabrics, but they could be. One of the quilts included is from a quilter who only makes scrap quilts from what she calls "real scraps." The fabric must be left over from something she or someone else has cut or from discarded fabric. She says that means her progress on scrap quilts moves more slowly, but she has a system that works for her.

My interpretation of what "scrap" means is much broader. I have a rather large collection of fabric and I feel that any fabric I didn't put in the last quilt becomes "leftover" or "scrap" fabric and qualifies for inclusion in the next scrap quilt.

Scrap quilts are not all quilts made from tiny pieces, but they can be tiny pieces. We call quilts made from thousands of tiny pieces Postage Stamp Quilts. They are often made from scraps, but not necessarily.

Not every piece in a scrap quilt need be a different fabric. However, when it is, we use the term "Charm Quilt" to denote that specific kind of scrap quilt. So while "charming" is one of the most frequently used adjectives when referring to scrap quilts, a charming quilt should not be confused with a Charm Quilt.

Some people use the expression "scrap quilts," even though they have collected laboriously and/or for a long period of time a wide variety of antique indigo prints or black and white prints or Hawaiian shirt prints or any of dozens of possible fabrics. I feel those quilts should be labeled, "Made from the painstakingly collected fabrics of _____." While they are made from many different fabrics, they really aren't scraps, but a specialty fabric collection.

It is always risky to name favorites, but no matter what else scrap quilts are, they are my favorite kind of quilt. Almost any quilting pattern or technique can be interpreted in scraps—this book does not pretend to cover every possibility. Your scrap quilts will look different from mine, because they will reflect your taste in fabrics over the years. That is one of the things that will make them special. If you are already making scrap quilts, I hope the quilts included here will give you new ideas. If you have never made a scrap quilt, I hope those here will provide the stimulus to begin.

WHY ARE SCRAP QUILTS SO POPULAR?

There are many reasons scrap quilts are so popular, but here are some of the most common influences.

Old-Time Reality

This was the original version of recycling. Think about it. If you had spun the threads, gathered the nuts to make the dye, dyed the threads and woven the fabric, would you throw away even the tiniest scrap? Or, let's say you were lucky and didn't have to spin and weave, but only had to drive the horse and buggy three hours to town to select from the twenty bolts of fabric at the General Store. This begins to explain why scrap quilts were popular a hundred years ago. We only had to look at some of the old ones to fall in love with them.

Ethics

The Puritan ethic and the Clean Plate Club have historically encouraged us to make something from nothing, and prompted us to develop an attitude that it is wasteful to throw anything away. "Use it up, wear it out, make it do or do without" was the philosophy many of us grew up with or heard from our grandparents.

Combining a waste-not, want-not ethic with the hoarding instincts some of us have when it comes to fabric, it's simple: We *have* to make scrap quilts.

Emotions

Garment scraps often hold very special memories. They recall the times and places a favorite dress was worn or the hours spent with Grandma the summer when she not only made the dress, but let you pick out the fabric. Sometimes the attachment to the fabric itself is what made the

dress so wonderful. Compiling those memories into quilts can be more satisfying than a photo album.

Like a lot of us who turn most of our textile time to quiltmaking, garment scraps may be a thing of the past. It is almost embarrassing to admit that I still attach the enjoyment of the moment of acquisition to the majority of my fabrics. Special stores, trips, trades, gifts from friends are all pleasant memories sewn into my quilts.

Self-satisfaction is another emotion sometimes released by making scrap quilts. Anyone who has rolled and saved and moved fabric scraps saying, "Someday, I'm going to make a quilt," can understand a feeling that falls between self-satisfied smugness and "I told you so." Actually using scraps collected over time can create a very self-satisfied feeling.

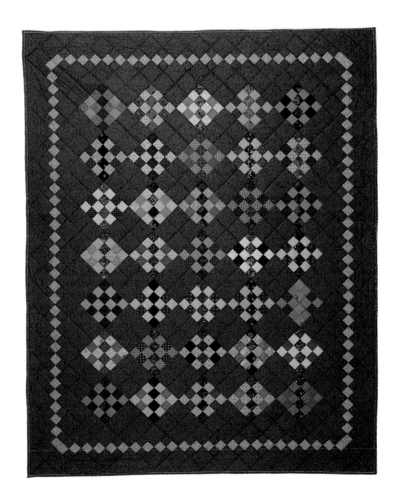

Using scraps can also be a great psychological release. At some point, each of us will say, "I just can't buy another piece of fabric until I use some of what I have." That expression verbalizes a feeling of guilt. Making a scrap quilt in such cases is a great mental release.

Not everyone understands this, but there is another thing I love about scrap quilts. Because they use a little bit of many different fabrics instead of a lot of a few fabrics, they rarely use the last piece of any of my favorite fabrics. There is always something left to fit into another quilt. This gives new meaning to the phrase "security blanket." If you ever just sit and play with your fabrics, even fondle them, you are likely to understand this appeal.

LOVING AND COLLECTING FABRICS

In our era, as fabrics have become very available and affluence more prevalent, there has been a great accumulation of fabric. We don't know when the first official fabric collection was begun, but we're convinced the 1980s and 1990s will go down in textile history as decades when many prominent fabric collections developed and, perhaps, when fabric collectors achieved a certain status. For the fabric collector, scrap quilts provide a two-fold attraction—a reason to have many fabrics and a way to use them. One of the real advantages of scrap quilts to a fabric collector is that scrap quilts require very small pieces of many different fabrics. That means I can buy ¾ yard of several different fabrics instead of having to decide on 3½ yards of just one fabric.

Just loving and collecting textiles is enough to get people into making scrap quilts. Conversely, if making scrap quilts becomes your specialty, that justifies the need for more fabric.

New Economics

At one time, scrap quilts conveyed a feeling of hand-me-down and were associated with being too poor to buy matching fabric. Things are now reversed, and scrap quilts are more likely to be regarded as a symbol of affluence. Modern scrap quilts often represent hours of shopping and a great personal collection of fabrics bought "just in case." A scrap quilt is one of the greatest ways to showcase a fabric collection.

Beauty

As a bonus, we discover that scrap quilts can be every bit as beautiful as more orderly quilts, and they are much more interesting.

CHAPTER 2

How to Collect Fabric Scraps

"HOW MUCH FABRIC DO I NEED?"

This is often the first question a fledgling quilt-maker asks. There is, of course, no single answer. How big a quilt you plan to make, what design you plan to use, and what variations you decide to incorporate as you go along all determine the answer.

The most important question with scrap quilts is really, "How many fabrics do I need?" To answer that question, we have included the approximate number of fabrics used in each project. However, these numbers are just a guideline; there is plenty of room for variation.

One of the beauties of scrap quilts is that in most cases it isn't necessary to have gathered together all of your fabric before you begin. If you have enough fabric to make just one block, you can start a scrap quilt.

"Don't Worry, I Have Enough Fabric!"

Many of you are reading this because you already have a lot of fabric and, I'm sure, at one time or other have felt guilty about your purchases. Because quilting is my vocation as well as avocation, I hear lots of fabric stories and I think I should share a few. The people involved will, of course, remain anonymous.

"My husband said, 'You've got to get this fabric out of here,' sooo, I just went down and rented a storage garage. I filled it with shelves and now when I finish shopping, I just go down and unload!"

"My husband said to me, 'Honey, how long does the fabric have to age before you can make it into a quilt?' " That question seemed so wonderful that several people, to whom I have told that story, now refer to their "fabric aging rooms" instead of their sewing rooms or studios.

I do know several quilters who have made secret pacts in case anything should happen to them. The pact is best established with someone who has similar taste and with whom you have done considerable shopping. It works like this: First, you agree to provide each other a complete list of all possible fabric hiding spots in your house. Second, you agree in case of the unforeseen, to rush to the other person's house, find and remove the fabric, and claim she was hiding all of it for you—to keep *your* family from knowing how much money you've really spent on fabric.

Personally, I take great offense at people who try to make fabric collectors feel guilty or apologetic. On the serious side, quilters must have a good selection of fabric. Unlike artists who work with paints and can mix any color they want, quilt artists are limited to working with the colors of fabric they have available. A great fabric collection should not be a source of guilt, but of pride—that is, as long as you are using it. Even I get upset with people who have a good fabric supply and then don't make quilts. Of course, people who collect stamps don't use them either, but I feel that the best use of a fabric collection is to combine those fabrics into quilts, and especially scrap quilts.

A Reverse Approach to Fabric Requirements

When I told a quilt guild in Nashville that I was writing a book on scrap quilts, they encouraged me to go see Nancy Granner's scrap quilts. It was really fun, because Nancy insists that the only fabrics that can go into scrap quilts must be "real" scraps. When she has some leftover fabric, she cuts it into several specific and commonly used shapes—two sizes of squares, two sizes of right triangles, and two sizes of equilateral triangles. She stores the shapes separately and when she has time to do a little piecing, the cutting is already done. Nancy selects commonly used shapes so she can piece many different blocks. She can decide when she starts to piece to continue making more blocks for an existing project or to experiment with a new design. When she has enough blocks to make something, she does. From her perspective, the object is to enjoy creating lovely new patchwork blocks from scraps, not to worry about how fast she can complete a quilt.

Nancy doesn't cut strips, but they are also an obvious shape to cut as you go. It would be easy to cut extra 1½-inch strips of any fabric you are using and store them away for a rainy day when making some Log Cabin blocks seems the best thing to do. Or cut 2-inch strips and make little four-patch sets.

"So, How Much Fabric Do I Need?"

It seems to me there are three approaches to decision-making when buying fabric—estimating, calculating, or collecting. If you estimate or calculate your needs for each quilt you make and never buy fabric speculatively, it may not be as much fun to make scrap quilts. If you are a collector, willing to buy speculatively or "just in case," you probably already have more than enough fabric to make a scrap quilt.

ACQUIRING ENOUGH SCRAPS

Of course, no one can define "enough." As one of my friends says, "You can never be too thin, too rich, or have too much fabric."

I am reminded of an evening when my husband and I were invited to join friends at a Chinese restaurant. In anticipation of eating out, I had "saved" calories all day. As we waited and even after dinner was served, our host kept repeating how huge the servings were and that no one could possibly finish them. I was intimidated into leaving half my dinner because I didn't want to be the only one to finish; then I went home hungry.

In the same way, if you don't have so much fabric that you feel compelled to hide it in the attic, I don't want you to be intimidated into thinking that you can't make scrap quilts. You *can* make scrap quilts, even if you don't have a huge stash of fabrics.

Organize a Fabric Exchange

It works on the same principle as a cookie exchange. Just as it is easier for one person to make ten dozen of the same cookie than a half dozen each of twenty cookies, it is easier for one person to cut forty strips or squares of the same fabric, or eighty triangles, or whatever. The best part is the resulting quilts won't look alike.

Be Creative

When Ellen Rosintoski agreed to participate in a quilt challenge, her biggest challenge was being limited to only eight fabrics. She loves to work with a multitude of fabrics so worked out a way to effectively turn those eight fabrics into twenty-five. (Her quilt and the instructions for it start on page 123.)

Many prints have very attractive wrong sides, especially for muted old-looking quilts. As you can see in the picture, Ellen's quilt is neither old or muted-looking, but she still used the wrong sides successfully.

Machine-stitching patterns onto fabric is another way to create an altogether different fabric. Ellen pre-embellished pieces of fabric with machine-stitched metallic threads and ribbon floss to add more texture and surface design to the fabrics. She also used both the front and back of some of the newly embellished fabrics.

Ellen did not dye any of her fabric scraps, but there is a time, place, and way to do that. The two most common ways of changing the color of fabric are tea dyeing and overdyeing.

Tea dyeing is very popular right now and is just what it says: using tea to change the color of the fabric. It is primarily used for aging, often to give a naturally stained, primitive look. While I sometimes tea-dye small craft projects, I am reluctant to tea-dye fabric for a quilt that I expect to wash and/ or keep a long time. The tea stains do gradually wash out, and we don't know the long-term effects of the acids in the tea on the fabric. Moreover, the colors obtainable with tea and coffee are limited and, if you want a lot of yardage with consistent coloring, you can't be very exact with repeat attempts.

Overdyeing gives more controllable results and has the advantage of a wide range of color choices. The best results will be achieved with cold-water *fiber-reactive* dyes on 100-percent cotton fabrics. The readily available all-purpose dye is not permanent enough for a long-lasting quilt.

Currently in craft and fabric stores you will find a large range of permanent fabric paints and dyes that are applied with a brush or tip applicator and can be used to create a greater variety in the fabrics you have. Read the instructions carefully and make a test piece before using it in a quilt.

Buy Creatively

Buying carefully from remnant bins and at sales will help you develop a more varied inventory.

Don't forget garage sales. Both used fabrics and fabrics that have never been used may be obtainable. It may seem silly, but it is difficult for me to cut up my own favorite used clothes, so I save them intact. On the other hand, I have no problem cutting quilt pieces from garments that absolute strangers are throwing away. In fact, I feel very noble rescuing those fabrics from certain landfill duty. As it may be more difficult to ascertain fiber content in second-hand garments, you should wash them before using, to assure shrinkage, color fastness, and washability.

Accept Gifts

Let people know you enjoy using scraps and you'll be amazed at how much fabric will be given to you. Don't forget to think about using the back of a fabric or embellishing or overdyeing fabrics. If non-quilters start sending over bags of fabric, begin to discriminate and eliminate fabrics you feel are completely unsuitable right away. Otherwise your house may be completely taken over with fabric.

Everyone has to make their own decision about what is acceptable. I'm almost positive I don't want to make a polyester double-knit quilt, for example, so I would send those scraps elsewhere. I'm absolutely positive I wouldn't want to use bonded acrylics from the late seventies. Silks, velveteen, and woolens, however, are fabrics I do enjoy working with, so I would keep them, but store them separately.

Maintaining and Storing Fabrics and Scraps

I would caution you about oversorting your larger pieces of fabric for storage. Certainly you want your fabrics in the same chest, closet, or room, depending on the space demands. Take fabrics out of sacks and fold or roll them similarly. Sort by fiber content. Then sort those that you have in abundance into general color families. Looking through generally sorted fabrics allows a lot more spontaneity in the selection of fabrics for scrap quilts. It amazes me how often fabrics that just happen to get put side by side when I am sorting and stacking and looking through my collection become the basis for a great block I would never have thought of otherwise.

Besides, where do you put multicolor fabrics? If you are looking for a blue and only look through your blue basket or pile, you will surely miss the perfect purple fabric with a blue design, tucked away inside the purple basket.

PREPARING SCRAPS FOR USE

Scraps will almost always need to be pressed, mainly to assure more accurate cutting.

What about preshrinking fabrics for scrap quilts? First, you need to understand that I belong to the camp that generally does *not* preshrink fabrics. I do test them. I know people who say—with an air of superiority, I might add—that they never walk in the door with fabric without immediately stopping at the washing machine and shrinking the fabric. I don't know people who really do that, but I have heard people say they do. If you are one of those who really does it, a big bonus is that your scraps are also preshrunk, and you can skip over the next few paragraphs.

The back of the pieced quilt top for the Ohio Star (see pages 90–95).

There are several reasons I don't routinely pre-shrink. In particular, I currently have a lot of un-used fabric, and if by chance it remains unused, I would have spent a lot of time shrinking fabric simply for the sake of shrinking. Frankly, that isn't at the top of the list of things I want to do for fun.

In addition, I mostly machine-piece and machine-quilt, so I prefer the crisp hand of fin-ished goods straight from the store. I feel they are easier to piece and quilt by machine. The crisp hand is lost in the first wash if you use hot water and detergent and double rinses. (I do want to point out, however, that friends of mine who do a lot of hand quilting say it is easier on their joints to remove that crispness.)

To me the look of unwashed fabrics is more appealing. It may be some time before a quilt needs to be washed, and I want to maintain that look as long as possible.

Because I basically am using familiar fabrics and small pieces, I admit to being a gambler in a lot of my scrap quilts. I don't even test little pieces. If you plan to hand-quilt or simply feel you must shrink every fabric, I would like to recommend this procedure:

Cut a piece slightly larger than what you want for the quilt. Put similar colors together and sim-ply put them in the last rinse cycle on your wash-ing machine. Use cold water. Then dry in the dry-er, but don't overdry. Press with a steam iron; if any of the fabrics are unusually limp, spray with sizing (not starch) when you press. It is not neces-sary to use any soap or detergent, as they do not promote shrinkage; they only help fade the colors. It is not necessary to use hot water in the washing machine. It is heat on the wet fibers that causes shrinkage. Your dryer will do that fine.

The one problem with this method is that it doesn't give you an opportunity to look at each fabric for color fastness. If you are not familiar with a fabric, you can dip a corner of your scrap into a large clear bowl and squeeze out excess water to look for any tell-tale bleeding of color. Lay aside any questionable fabric and test more carefully. It may be necessary to wash fabrics separately until there is no sign of bleeding or running color.

"BUT HOW MUCH FABRIC DO I REALLY NEED?"

There really isn't an answer to this question when you are making scrap quilts. For example, you can't even think of calling a full-size quilt a scrap quilt if it doesn't include at least forty different fabrics.

A wonderful thing about scrap quilts is that you don't have to calculate much yardage. Using a single fabric as a border or as the constant for the control factor does require a specific amount of fabric, but otherwise, how much of any given fabric you use in a quilt is very flexible.

There is a rule of thumb for total yardage on a quilt top. Start by understanding that 6 yards of 45-inch-wide fabric, cut in half crosswise and seamed once along the selvages, will give you a piece approximately 89 by 108 inches. That is almost a perfect size backing for many queen/double quilts. Now begin to allow extra for seams. The smaller the pieces, the more seams there will be in a quilt top. Allow extra for directional cutting or special positioning of a printed design in the patchwork shape. Allow extra for variety and extra for options. It is easy to see why most queen/double quilt tops will take 10 to 12 actual yards of fabric.

Following the same thought process, allow 7 to 8 yards for a twin and 12 to14 yards for a king-size quilt top.

Ad Lib Scrap Quilts

Please remember that every quilt doesn't have to be made for a bed! Many of the quilts in this book are for the wall or crib, or are blocks turned into smaller projects. You can start something and change your mind. Often things take on a different look than you thought they would. Don't keep forcing yourself to finish a full-size quilt when it would make more sense to stop and make a small wall hanging or try another idea for the quilt.

If you have miscalculated, the wonderful thing about scrap quilts is that you can just ad lib! My favorite ad lib is, "When you run out of fabric, you know how big your quilt will be."

Last Words About "How Much" Fabric

We are only listing batting and backing requirements in the "Quilt-As-You-Sew" chapter, because you must have the needed amount to start a quilt using the quilt-as-you-sew technique. Otherwise Chapter 11 provides information about quilt backs (my favorites are also made from scraps), borders, bindings, etc. With scrap quilts there are so many options.

If you do have 2½- to 3½-yard pieces of fabric in your collection, remember to save a wide section along one selvage for potential border and binding strips. They are best cut on the lengthwise grain and not pieced.

All fabric requirements given in yards refer to fabrics that are 45 inches wide.

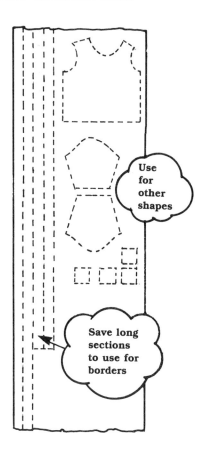

Use for other shapes

Save long sections to use for borders

Metric Conversion Chart

1 meter = 39.37 inches
1 inch = 2.54 cms.
Yards × .9144 = meters
Inches × 2.54 = cms.

Understanding Your Scraps

Most people, even when they love the look of scrap quilts, find putting them together is still an acquired skill. And this is particularly the case with fabric selection. If you were born before 1970, you probably recall your mother saying, "You can't wear that flowered blouse with that plaid skirt!" It must have been in the 1970s that we began to put two coordinating prints together. The key word here is "coordinating," because free-ranging combinations still weren't highly regarded. The point is that putting lots of prints together is a retraining process for most people because we have been taught not to put prints together.

Perhaps the most important thing to do is to begin thinking of your fabrics in many more ways than just in terms of color or fiber. But in order to do that, we must still first think about the fiber and color.

SORTING YOUR FABRICS

Sort by Fiber

One-hundred-percent cotton is the fiber of choice for quilts. You can fairly safely combine some cotton/polyester blends and still have washability, but most quilters prefer using 100-percent cotton.

For now, let's look at cotton prints. Sort through your fabrics for cottons. Stack the solid colors separately. It would be great to have at least forty cotton prints to start playing with.

Sort by Hue

Now sort by hue or color name, the way most quilt shops arrange their fabrics. The first time you sort by hue, use the ROY G BIV method. That acronym is the way I learned to remember the order of the colors of the spectrum: red, orange, yellow, green, blue, indigo, violet.

Then add a pile for neutrals: white, black, ecru,

gray, beige. The gray and beige neutrals can usually be positioned at the very lightest end of a color or hue.

As you look at individual stacks of fabric, you may discover that some piles are overflowing and that you want to subdivide them. Or you may note that you don't even own some of the colors. That means you are working with a limited palette.

So that you can begin to relate to fabrics in different ways, sort them again by each category that is discussed.

Warm and Cool

This is pretty easy once you have your fabrics sorted by color. Typically, the red, yellow, and orange groups are warm like the sun, and the blue, green, and violet groups are cool like a forest. But it isn't always that easy. Some purples are decidedly warm, heavy with red tones, while others are very cool. What about the neutrals? They usually include fabrics that appear decidedly warm or cool.

Light, Medium, and Dark

Value is the lightness or darkness of a color. When you are making scrap quilts, I believe that light, medium, and dark are more important characteristics than red, blue, and yellow. In color terminology, we would say that value is more important than the hue.

Go through and restack your fabrics in these three categories. It is not as easy as it sounds. Generally, the fabrics in the light pile would all *look* light compared to those in the dark pile. There would be lots of contrast, as in black and white or dark gray and light gray. These fabrics would also look light compared to those in the medium pile, but there wouldn't be as much contrast. Likewise, the medium pile would be lighter than the dark pile, but there again you wouldn't see as much contrast.

If you were working with only eight or ten fabrics, the same fabric could be a medium in one small group of fabrics and a dark in the next. It is all relative or "compared to" as a reference. You may have discovered that your personal scraps do, in fact, reflect a personal bias for or against very light or dark fabrics. Whatever the case, if you are shopping specifically for fabrics for your quilts, it is important to buy a variety of values as well as a variety of hues.

It might be fun to try to put all forty fabrics you have in order from lightest to darkest. Another good exercise is to sort each hue by value—that is, each color from lightest to darkest.

If you were to sort all your fabrics on a scale from 1 to 10, with the lightest being 1 and darkest 10, then arbitrarily say you aren't going to use any

fabric lighter than 4, 4 becomes a light fabric in the quilt even though it had been a medium. There would, however, be less contrast.

High or low contrast within a single fabric is also important to consider. A single fabric with very high contrast in its print can be very distracting within the quilt. The higher the contrast, the busier the fabric looks. The greater the print's contrast, the farther away it can be seen. That means it is not only distracting close up, but from across the room.

Size or Scale of Design

At this point, sorting by size—very small, small, medium, large, and very large—would be enough, but it would also be fun to go from the smallest print to the largest. It is very important to have a good variety of different scales of design in the fabrics that you will put into a scrap quilt.

It is a common misconception that only tiny little prints can be used in quilts. I believe the most successful use of very small prints is to replace solids.

Cutting small pieces from a very large print can give the illusion of many different fabrics, and often the actual motif is completely lost in the cutting and only a wonderful swirl of color remains.

Density of Design

Very closely related to the size or scale is the density of the design. How much background color is allowed to show through? Is it a solid plain color or is there texture, as with a random dot pattern? Are there big empty areas of background and then large design areas, or are the design areas evenly distributed. Maybe the fabric features lots of design, with only a little background peeking through.

Random or Rigid Design

Random design means there is no order whatever in the designs used in the fabric. Where there is a distinctive order to the designs, we speak of rigid design. The most common rigid designs are stripes, and/or a check or plaid that has even rows repeating consistently.

Random designs are always less restrictive than rigid, but they can't be used to direct your eye the way a stripe can.

While random designs are easier to use and less likely to surprise you, you do not have to avoid rigid designs; just respect them. If you are trying to make scrap quilts with an antique look, you will want to incorporate rigid designs, as they were very common in quilts from 1875 to 1920.

Directional Designs

Look through your fabrics to determine if there are any with directional designs. The most obvious would be a stripe, but fabrics with all the flower heads going in one or two directions are also directional. "Tossed" is usually the opposite of directional.

Calm to Busy

Generally, fabrics that are designed with low contrast, only two colors, delicate design, and small scale are considered calm; the opposite would be considered busy. Look at your fabrics and pick some of each. Stand back at least six feet and see if your choices would be different.

Mood or Theme

The mood you are trying to create will be the final deciding factor in whether a questionable fabric should be included. A high-contrast, large-scale design that is out of place in a romantic turn-of-the-century style quilt can be perfect for a very contemporary scrap quilt.

CONTRAST AS A DESIGN TOOL

By its very nature, contrast is an important element of patchwork design. If there isn't contrast between pieces, the patchwork patterns don't develop or aren't visible. The degree of contrast can vary greatly, but there must be some.

Contrast can be developed in many different ways. Almost all of the headings preceding this one in this chapter are really discussions of contrast. Keep in mind also that clashing and "surprise" fabrics used together may also provide dramatic contrast. High-contrast items sprinkled through a quilt can really keep your eyes interested; they make the quilt top sparkle.

Fabric Cautions

Almost any fabric can be included in a scrap quilt, but that does not mean any fabric can go in any quilt. Everyone has to make their own decisions, but some of the fabrics that can surprise you in a scrap quilt are:

• Fabrics with very high contrast
• Fabrics with very intense and bright colors
• Fabrics with many clear colors
• Fabrics of unusual fibers or weaves

Fabric other than medium-weight cotton should be used with caution and concern for consistency in stitching, washability, and quiltability.

HOW TO KEEP SCRAP QUILTS UNDER CONTROL

As you begin to look at the quilts in this book and, I hope, as you look at all scrap quilts with a more understanding eye, one of the things I'm sure you will discover is that the quilts that really work incorporate some degree of control. Something ties the wide variety of fabrics together. There are many different approaches, and they will be pointed out as we go along, but for starters, think about:

• A common background fabric. Often muslin is used to unite a variety of colors. (See the Little English Lady, page 107). This is especially appropriate when making 1920s-looking scrap quilts. Otherwise, my preference is something with a little more punch. My favorite is an assortment of light-value, small-scale prints that read like muslin from a distance but show more texture and variety of the fabric assortment as you get up close (see World Without End, page 117).

The Full-Size Blue Mosaic on page 64 uses the blue alternating blocks of one fabric in this way. It also uses the common fabric in the four-patches around the border as a control element.

• A common multicolor print fabric can be used to develop the color scheme, as in the Quilt-As-You-Sew Ohio Star, page 90.

• Almost any quilt design that is effective as a positive–negative quilt will be effective as a scrap quilt. Just divide scraps into light and dark and proceed.

• Use lots of different prints. It really does seem that the more different prints there are, the easier it is to put them together. When I started to pull the purple fabrics for Helen's Purple Fans (see page 100), nothing looked right when I tried to confine the fabrics to just the reddish purples. The same was true when I decided to go with just the blue tones. When I finally just decided to work with all the purples, it was wonderful.

• Repetition of an accent color can be very controlling. Look at Illusions on page 55. Your eye follows the accent to develop a strong design.

• A limited palette can be effective. One example is the Quilt-As-You-Sew Pinwheel Log Cabin, page 85, worked with the red, rust, green, gold, brown, and ecru palette.

• Likewise, a limited range of values puts a degree of control into a quilt. Bettina Havig's Mariner's Compass on page 126 incorporates a limited range of values and a common background fabric.

The list here in no way claims to cover all of the ways to control a scrap quilt. Learn to look at quilts that you like and analyze what made them pleasing to you.

Use the quilts in this book and others as inspiration. But stay flexible. No matter how much you love something you see, it is unrealistic to try to find exactly the same fabrics and colors so that you can duplicate another quilt faithfully.

SPECIAL "AGING" CONSTRUCTION TIPS

Many people especially enjoy making scrap quilts with an antique look, but then don't think to follow traditional practices. Here are some tips derived from studying many old scrap quilts.

• Piece colors or fabrics within a shape. It was very common on old quilts for fabric to be pieced in order to be large enough for a particular triangle or square.
• Cut some pieces off grain. For those of us drilled in cutting fabrics on grain, the thought of purposely cutting off grain is difficult at best. To convince yourself, study the old quilts you love and see if you don't discover many off-grain pieces.
• Don't overmatch. One of the easiest mistakes is to overmatch right into boredom.
• Don't get overpretty. If you look closely at fabrics in a scrap quilt you love, don't be surprised to find real ugly fabrics and ugly combinations. Incorporating ugly pieces is hard to do, but often necessary to keep a quilt from being boring.
• You may even want to age fabrics artificially, such as washing them to give a puckered and aged look. Another technique is to overdye or tea-dye prints for an aged look (see page 13).
• Consider using cotton batting. The most popular batting today is polyester, but cotton batting gives a different, more authentic look if you are trying to make a quilt that looks old. Don't forget that *cotton batting must be quilted more closely than polyester* to keep from balling up when it is washed. Many machine quilters are finding that they enjoy quilting on cotton and that the heavy density of quilting is not nearly as time-consuming by machine as by hand.
• If you have or secure authentic old fabric and carefully select the new fabrics to go with it, the old look is even more convincing.

A quilt isn't done until it is signed and dated, especially if you are striving to make a quilt with an 1895 look in 1995. Please sign and date it.

CHAPTER 4

Getting Started

HOW LONG WILL IT TAKE TO MAKE A QUILT?

Just as we can't tell you exactly how much fabric it will take to make a quilt, we can't tell you how much time it will take. The actual quilt you decide to make, your skill level, whether you sew by hand or machine, and whether you work for long stretches or do a lot of stop-and-start sewing will greatly affect the amount of time it takes to finish the quilt.

The emphasis in this book is on making it easy for you to get started with scrap quilts. The quilts selected are all very doable, without your having to sacrifice design. There are special sections on strip techniques and machine quilting. The Quilt-As-You-Sew chapter turns anyone who knows how to use a sewing machine into a quiltmaker, with no quilting frame or hoops required. At the same time there is recognition that hand piecing, scrap quilts, and a more leisurely pace are comfortable companions. The choice is up to you.

TOOLS

If you have done much sewing or quilting, most of the tools you will need are probably already in your sewing supplies—good small scissors, a seam ripper, thimbles, a new packet of needles, etc. You may also want to add some specialized quilting tools, like erasable fabric-marking pens and pencils, small acrylic rulers, and acrylic squares for use with rotary cutters. Put a steam iron and ironing board next to your sewing machine.

MARKING AND CUTTING

You should decide whether you are going to piece by hand or machine *before* you mark and cut. If you are going to piece by machine, you will probably mark the cutting lines and approximate the seam lines as you sew (easily done on most sewing machines). Conversely, most hand-piecers will mark the sewing lines and then approximate the seam allowance as they cut, or they may mark both lines.

Your fabric scraps will determine the best way to proceed from here. If you are using small bits and pieces of many fabrics, you may find you need to mark your shapes and cut them individually. If you have larger pieces, you may be able to take advantage of the rotary cutting method, which lets you measure and cut at the same time to speed up the process and get on with the fun.

Rotary Cutting Method

One of the greatest advantages of this method is the accuracy and precision you gain in your cutting, which is crucial to accurate patchwork. Rotary cutting also lets you quickly cut multiple layers all at once, and saves time in measuring. Along with the rotary cutter you will need a protective mat and a strong straight-edge to cut along. There are many different acrylic rulers available, 5 or 6 inches wide and 24 inches long, and they are well worth the investment. The grid on the ruler surface lets you measure without marking and keeps your cutting accurate.

Most of the instructions in this book will refer to the rotary cutting method, but if you are chained to your scissors you can still use patterns and markings to cut everything. However, you will never achieve the ease and accuracy that comes with the rotary cutter. If you have never used a rotary cutter, I assure you that once you try it, you will never want to do without it. You'll be hooked!

THREAD

All-cotton and cotton-wrapped polyester are the sentimental thread favorites and logical to use against cotton fibers. Many people feel the stronger 100-percent polyester threads will, given enough time, cut the cotton fibers in the fabric. If you decide to piece and quilt by machine, you will use lots of thread, but don't be tempted by cheap thread. In most cases, sewing with a matching color is not important. You can sometimes find large spools of natural colors that will save money without compromising quality.

For machine quilting I often use a very fine transparent nylon thread on the top of my machine, with regular sewing thread in the bobbin. Quilting thread is a heavier, often waxed-feeling thread, reserved for hand quilting. (More about quilting in Chapter 11.)

SEAM ALLOWANCE

The recommended seam allowance for piecing is ¼ inch, but in the final analysis, it's the size of what you see that is really important, not the size of the seam allowance. The objective is to have a perfect 2-inch square, for example, not a perfect ¼-inch seam allowance. *Most measurements given in this book are cut measurements.*

Pressing Seams

Pressing is not optional. Time spent carefully pressing is time well spent; you should make your iron one of your best friends. When pressing seams in patchwork, both seam allowances go in the same direction, not open as in dressmaking. A general rule to follow is to press toward the darker side. After you have pressed the seam to one side, turn it over and press again on the right side to make sure you can eliminate any tiny folds you might have pressed into the seam. Tiny ¹⁄₃₂-inch folds don't seem like much until you multiply that times two for each seam, times four or five seams for a block, and times ten or twelve for the number of blocks!

PUTTING IT ALL TOGETHER

Try different methods. Remember we aren't into rights and wrongs with this, but making your own choice and enjoying!

Hand-Piece/Hand-Quilt

This is a very portable quilt-making approach. Some people find hand work very soothing. Some people consider this the most "authentic" way to make a quilt. If you are trying to reproduce an antique hand-made quilt, it is, but that is not the only way to make a "real" quilt.

Machine-Piece/Hand-Quilt

As soon as the sewing machine was invented, it was regularly used for piecing quilts, but not as frequently for quilting, so many current quilters consider a machine-pieced and hand-quilted quilt to be "authentic." In many museums and quilt shows, I have learned that machine quilting was done as soon as sewing machines were invented, but mostly on quilts that were in daily use. I'm convinced that many women chose to machine-piece tops but would wait and hand-quilt in a group. Quilting was a very social thing and afforded one of the few opportunities to spend a day with other women talking about the things women talk about. Who would want to give that up just because she was lucky enough to have acquired a sewing machine?

Machine-Piece/Machine-Quilt

This is my personal method of choice, mainly because it allows me to complete more quilts. If I had more time, I would do more hand quilting, because it is pleasant to do and the results beautiful to see. But I am very comfortable using the sewing machine and consider it an ally, sometimes a genius.

(A special form of machine piecing and machine quilting is explained in the section called Quilt-As-You-Sew, starting on page 85.)

Machine-Piece/Combined Machine and Hand Quilting

More and more, people find the combined use of machine and hand quilting to be a logical response to different needs. They will machine-quilt "in the ditch" around large unit blocks and border seams and then come back and hand-quilt inside the blocks. That approach lets the machine do the long, tedious, but necessary stitching, and the hand work is done where it will show to best advantage.

Hand-Piece/Machine-Quilt

It's possible, but I don't know anyone who does it and can't imagine why anyone would.

HAND-PIECING TIPS

Personally, I do lots more machine piecing than hand piecing, but I have friends who say they hand-piece because they can carry the work along easily or because they tense up at the machine.

Several of my friends say their husbands are happier if they spend their evenings together in the family room instead of separated, with her in the sewing room and him in the family room. One eloquently adds that she isn't sure why he finds it so comforting to sleep in front of the TV with her watching, but she obliges as much as possible between stitches.

There is a little saying:

By the yard, life is hard;
By the inch, it's a cinch!

That surely could be applied to hand-piecing a quilt.

It is amazing how quickly you can complete one section and then another, just stitching along. It is important to remember that hand piecing creates a softer seam, and much more forgiveness. For example, you can ease one piece more than another; you can manipulate intricate corners. But keep in mind that many people who hand-piece blocks do set them together and add borders with the sewing machine.

Hand piecing and scrap quilts can be especially compatible (see "A Reverse Approach to Fabric Requirements," page 11). Precut scraps and hand piecing in the family room can be a perfect combination.

Needles

I often read that people like #10 Betweens. When I'm doing hand piecing, I want a little more needle to grasp, so I use #7 Betweens or sometimes Sharps. Betweens are short and stubby. Sharps are longer and more tapered. The larger the number, the smaller the needle.

Decide for yourself, but whatever you choose, get a package, and thread at least six at one time. I would say to thread the whole package, but that sounds outrageous. Once you see how advantageous it is to thread lots of needles at one time, instead of stopping to handle the spool, scissors, etc., each time, you'll probably decide to do that on your own.

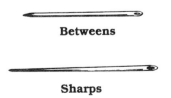

Betweens

Sharps

Thread

Length: Not too long—20 to 25 inches seems about right. I hear lots of people say 18 inches, but that seems to go so fast. I think they say 18 inches because they know everyone will cut the thread a little longer.

Cut: Remember to slant your sharp scissors so that the cut on the thread is actually diagonal. That way the thread will go through the eye of the needle more easily. If you are having to try several times to get the thread through the eye, don't be stubborn about resorting to a needle threader. It can save so much time, time spent much more enjoyably piecing or quilting than trying to thread a needle.

Color: Choose color-matched thread if you are piecing lots of same-color fabric, but a good neutral is fine for piecing scraps.

Quality: Only use *good* thread. Forget about the cheap sale spools.

Beeswax: Some people like to run their thread across the edge of a piece of beeswax. They feel that makes it go through the material more easily, perhaps more for quilting than piecing.

Seam Allowance

Until you feel comfortable eye-balling the ¼-inch width of the seam allowance, marking the seam line is probably worth the effort. Hand piecers often mark both the cutting lines and sewing lines. That is always worth the effort on curved seams or complicated patterns. It is especially important to mark the ends of a seam.

Intersections

It is nice to leave seam allowances at intersections loose to facilitate directional pressing. This is a technique that machine piecers cannot do as easily as hand piecers. I know some hand piecers who only sew between seam allowances and never cross a seam allowance. I usually cross the first seam allowance and then leave that seam allowance unstitched when I would normally be crossing it on the next seam.

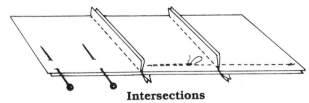

Intersections

Stitching

The two most common stitches for hand piecing are the straight continuous running stitch and the back stitch. But let's first discuss the very first stitch.

No, no, no! Don't knot the thread. Take a tiny stitch on top of a tiny stitch to secure the thread at both the beginning and end of a seam. Remember, the softer hand is one of the advantages of hand piecing. Don't ruin it with a big bulky knot. Believe it or not, pun intended, some knots are so big they can, with time, actually wear a hole in the fabric.

No knots!

Backstitch from tiny overlapping stitches at beginning (right).

Continuous Running Stitch, Straight Seam

Weave as many small stitches on the needle as you can before pulling the needle through the fabric. Try pulling the thread just a few inches so that you have room to manipulate your needle and thread and weave stitches on again. Now pull the thread all the way through the stitches and start again. By eliminating as many long pulls as possible, you speed up the progress. As you are developing the rhythm of your stitch, be cautious about your stitch tension. Do not pull too tightly, so that the fabric gathers, or not tight enough so that the stitches aren't smooth.

**Running stitch
(straight seam)**

Continuous Running Stitch, Curved Seam

You can't expect to weave as many stitches on the needle with a curved seam as with a straight seam; otherwise it is the same process.

**Running stitch
(curved seam)**

Back Stitch

Back stitch almost seems like a misnomer, because it starts by going farther forward and then coming back and overlapping. On the reverse side you get an overlapping line of thread.

Back stitch

MACHINE-PIECING TIPS

The Machine

Don't panic. You don't need a fancy machine. All you need is one that stitches forward. Back stitching is rarely needed, because most seams are secured at the end by being sewn into the next seam. The tension must be properly adjusted. If it isn't, you can get puckered seams (tension is too tight) or fabrics actually pull apart and stitches show through on the right side of the seam (tension is too loose).

If you haven't used your machine in a while, dust it off, oil it, clean out the lint, and put in a new needle (size 14/90). It doesn't matter that the needle isn't bent. If you can't remember changing it, it's too dull for this work. Thread your machine and adjust the tension. Read your owner's manual for help.

Stitching

Ten to twelve stitches per inch is nice for piecing. On many sewing machines, the outside edge of the presser foot is exactly ¼ inch from the center of the needle hole, conveniently the same width as our seam allowances need to be. This lets you accurately place your seams without having to mark the actual seam line. An easy way to check your machine is to put a tape measure under your presser foot. Put any inch mark at the needle and put the presser foot down. If it is ¼ inch wide, you're lucky. If it isn't, you'll have to find some way to calculate the ¼-inch seam. Many of the new sewing machines have adjustable needle positions, so you may be able to correct the position very easily.

When you are getting ready to start sewing, take a minute to wind about six bobbins. This lets you keep going without having to stop and rewind a bobbin in the middle of a seam, a frustrating exercise at best.

Techniques

As you work through the projects included in this book, you will find many more ideas on methods such as strip piecing and chain piecing, which are simply easy ways of using your sewing machine to speed up the piecing process. Look for them and give them a try. They will let you speed through some of the more repetitious tasks and move on to more enjoyable things.

WHAT IS DIFFERENT ABOUT MAKING SCRAP QUILTS?

If you have been making quilts, it would be fair to ask, "Why the fuss about scrap quilts?" or "What would be any different?"

Working with so many fabrics in one quilt is what creates the difference.

- *Expect a slow start.* We've already covered collecting the fabrics, and what that entails, in Chapter 2. The extended effort it takes to build a fabric stockpile is often underestimated. Some people feel this is actually a real advantage. They select quilt designs conducive to collecting and piecing as time goes by. Whenever they have enough units pieced to make a quilt, they do so, but their scrap quilts have no other deadlines.

Another approach is to cut for several quilts from the same scrap pile. It is easy to make them look different. (For an explanation of this, see the sidebar on page 118.)
- *Scrap quilts disturb quick-cutting and strip-piecing techniques.* It is important to note the

word "disturb." You don't have to give up completely the new techniques you've learned with rotary cutting systems, chain piecing, etc. However, those techniques will not offer the same efficiency in scrap quilts as they do with quilts made from three fabrics. Because I am personally such an advocate of these techniques, I've included a separate chapter on this subject (see Chapter 7)!
- *There are more decisions.* With every fabric you have to decide whether or not to use it, what to combine it with, where to place pieces of it in the finished quilt, and so on. You should be prepared for that. It is also crucial to remember that these decisions are not a matter of life or death. I feel a relaxed attitude is a requirement if you are to enjoy making scrap quilts.
- *Scrap quilts generally demand a big floor.* If you are making a quilt with a single repetitive block, once you've decided on the block, you may want to double-check that you still like the arrangement of fabrics when you combine the first four blocks. You don't have to lay out thirty blocks before you study positioning. However, almost all scrap quilts will need to be laid out on the floor and studied and changed and studied and changed again. This is something you could do forever if you don't relax. You are just looking for a comfortable balance: Are there too many blue parts clumped together? Are all the large-scale designs in one corner? Does it matter which direction the stripes go?

With quilts that have alternating solid blocks, as in the Mosaic quilts, you may well change your choice of alternating fabrics or decide to change the border plan once the quilt is laid out on the floor.
- *Scrap quilts are warmer.* Some people laugh at me, but I insist it's true. It must be because these quilts exude warmth and memories from the design surface in addition to the expected thermal warmth. If you don't believe that, you will surely agree that scrap quilts are happy quilts. They are not pretentious, they make you want to linger.

CHAPTER 5

String Quilting

"String quilting" or "string piecing" is the traditional name for using assorted narrow strips of fabrics in quilt pieces. "Stitch and flip," a phrase used today, is more explicit in describing the technique. It is a fascinating way to use up the smallest pieces of fabric. If you don't have thin strips of fabric, you can always cut strips from sections of fabric. They can be cut parallel with a constant width, parallel with random widths, or irregular. I prefer irregular widths most of the time.

Most people do the construction on a base material. How that is done will be easier to understand once you read the instructions for a specific project.

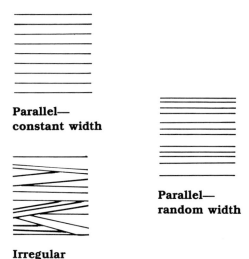

Parallel— constant width

Parallel— random width

Irregular

Red, White, and Blue String Quilt

Circa 1900–1910

APPROXIMATE FINISHED SIZE:
   70 × 84 inches

MATERIALS REQUIRED:
   Equivalent of 10–12 yards of fabric for top
   Base material of choice

You will notice that this is called the Red, White, and Blue String Quilt, which implies using only scraps that are in those three color groups. I specifically bought this quilt to illustrate a point: You can often include other colors even when focusing on a set color scheme. While the impression this quilt gives is of a red, white, and blue color scheme, upon closer examination you will see that it is full of lavender fabric.

If I were selecting fabrics for this quilt now, I would push the color barriers by using *any* blue, from baby to periwinkle to navy. I would not include the lavender, but might throw in a dark teal or plum or brown for a surprise fabric. I would incorporate any red, but use limited quantities of bright reds and bright orange-reds, and I'd use a lot of ecru instead of white. The quilt shown includes more than sixty different fabrics.

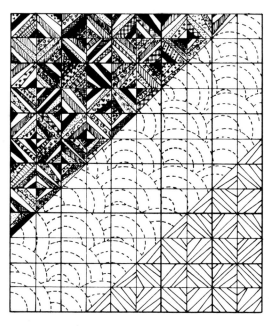

Figure 1: Red, White, and Blue String Quilt with quilting pattern

Making the Blocks

1. Select the scraps you want to work with.

2. Cut disposable or removable base materials (tear-away background stabilizer, freezer paper, or paper—see box) the finished size of the chosen shape, in this case a 7-inch square. Seam allowances will be added later. The base material will be much easier to tear away if it isn't caught in the next seam. If you are going to make the full-size quilt shown, you will need 120 squares.

  If you are using a fabric base that will not be removed, such as prewashed muslin, you will probably prefer to cut it with seam allowances included and trim scraps to match.

3. Select your first two strips of scrap. For the large quilt they are placed right sides together and positioned diagonally across the center of the base square. The three layers are positioned at the

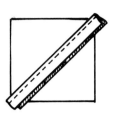
Figure 2

Figure 3

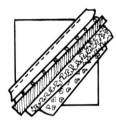
Figure 4

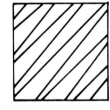
Figure 5

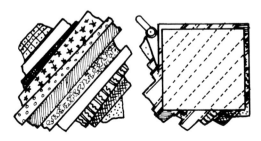
Figure 6   **Figure 7**

sewing machine with the base material on the bottom. Stitch along the edge of the two fabric strips in line with the corners (Figure 2). It is important that the stitching line be very straight. Curves in the stitching will not allow the strips to open flat. Short straggling ends of scraps are allowed to hang off the edge of the base for now. Trimming comes later.

4. Open the two fabric strips just stitched and press them flat (Figure 3). Place the next strip face down on one raw edge and stitch again. Stitch and flip, stitch and flip, as often as necessary (Figure 4). This will be determined both by the size of the base piece and the width of the scraps.

To speed things along, try to work on both halves of many base pieces before stopping to press.

TIP: When working with irregular strips, they will tend to radiate from a point if all of the narrow ends are on the same side of the square. This is sometimes very effective, but if you want to prevent that, alternate the narrow ends (Figure 5).

5. When the surface of the base material is covered (Figure 6), it is time to trim away excess scrap fabric, and at the same time create the seam allowances (Figure 7).

In the old days, the base material, which was often newspaper, seemed to include the seam allowances and that material was either sewn into the seam or removed before the process of joining blocks. To remove the base material now would eliminate the benefit of stability and increase the risk of stretching the blocks. Sewing the base material into the seams makes it more difficult to remove.

Using the base material as your guide, cut the sewn fabrics ¼ inch larger all around. This is especially easy with a rotary cutting system. Lay the sewn piece fabric side down on a rotary cutting mat. Line up an acrylic ruler so that it extends ¼ inch beyond the base and trim away the excess.

Putting the Blocks Together

To finish a full-size quilt like the one shown, now arrange the blocks and sew them together. Because there are so many blocks, it will be easier if you first sew them into sets of four, with the diagonals alternating as illustrated (Figure 8). Then it is best to do a full layout on the floor to balance your colors and fabrics. When satisfied, finish sewing the units in pairs, pairs of pairs, etc.

Finishing the Quilt

The quilting pattern used on the antique quilt shown is often referred to as the Baptist Fan (look back to Figure 1). The story is that the arc comes from the top of the old paper fans handed out in church on sultry summer Sundays. It's a good story, but I learned how to do this design with a pencil and string. This pattern is one of the simplest to use to practice quilting in a frame, because you are always quilting in a gradual arc toward yourself. This is probably why it was so often used by women's church circle quilting groups. It is easy to mark, easy to quilt, and moves very quickly. The pattern is so simple that I've heard Baptist women call it the Methodist Fan,

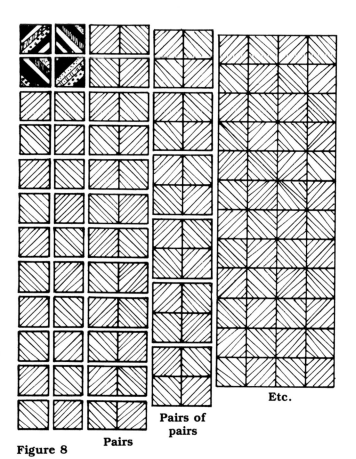

Etc.

Pairs of pairs

Pairs

Figure 8

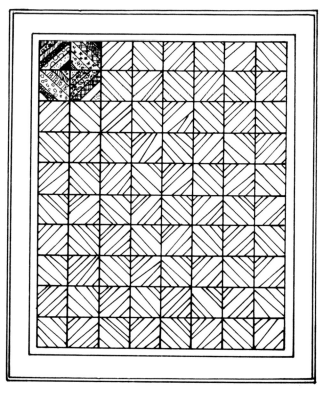

Figure 9

to prevent anyone from thinking they had to have a quilting pattern that easy!

Layer, quilt as desired, and bind with a separate ¾-inch finished binding. (See Chapter 11 for details.)

ALTERNATE IDEAS

Alternate layouts may go faster. If a project with 120 blocks seems too ambitious, try eighty 10-inch squares. (Figure 9 shows eighty 8-inch squares with 10-inch total borders.) If you do change the number of squares, remember to keep an even number of rows so that you can develop the pattern in sets of four string-pieced blocks.

A More Controlled Piecing Method

The Red, White, and Blue String Quilt is quite spontaneous. The diagonal positioning of the strips, with an apparent attempt to make a corner-to-corner diagonal seam, is the only consistent feature of the design.

You can ensure more orderly positioning via a construction technique that adds considerable control to the quilt design: Imagine that each square has a diagonal line drawn on the back of the paper base (Figure 10). When sewing the marked back, position the base

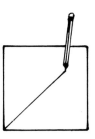

Figure 10

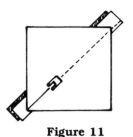

Figure 11

Figure 12

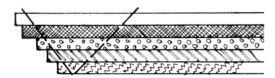

Figure 13

Figure 1: Rotary Mat Satchel

material on top, marked side up, with the fabric strips underneath, right sides together. This is just the reverse of the first method.

Do not expect even seam allowances. These are scraps. Just make sure that both pieces of fabric that are to be sewn to the base extend beyond the drawn line (Figure 11). When you turn the base over to press the strips open, check the seam allowances and trim away any excess. There will be a perfect diagonal line on each piece.

What if the first two strips are always one red and one blue? Nothing else is consistent—not the width of the strips or the specific fabrics used. Then when the sets of blocks are combined, you can arrange them to get nice alternating blue and red squares, sitting on point. With that technique, you add even more control to the string piecing.

String Piecing Without a Base Material

Sometimes people can get the same effect by string-piecing large strips of material and then cutting shapes from the resulting scrap yardage. This is sometimes referred to as strip piecing. It is faster because you have eliminated a base piece and don't stop and start at each edge of the base piece. Look at the two triangles that make up the twelve squares in the Rotary Mat Satchel which follows. Would you prefer to cut a separate little strip for every piece of the triangle and then stop and start to sew them together (Figure 12), or sew several longer strips together and cut the triangle from the sewn fabric (Figure 13)?

The string or strip piecing might be parallel strips of consistent width, parallel strips of random width, or irregular strips. There are appropriate uses for all three.

Rotary Mat Satchel

APPROXIMATE SIZE:
   18 × 24 inches

MATERIAL REQUIREMENTS:
   Fifty 1½ × 22½-inch strips, twelve to twenty-five assorted fabrics
   ⅝ yard fabric for back and handles
   1⅛ yards fabric for lining and handles
   1⅛ yards polyester fleece

The Rotary Mat Satchel shown (Figure 1) is for carrying your own 18 by 24-inch rotary mat, rotary cutter, and any acrylic templates to sewing or quilting classes. It is convenient and good protection for your tools, plus a fun little scrap project. On one patchwork side it has twelve 6-inch squares. The color scheme was selected to harmonize with the green mat. The strips are of even width, in this case, 1 inch finished.

Selecting and Cutting the Fabric Strips

As discussed in Chapter 3, "Understanding Your Scraps," select a good variety of colors, scale, and tone. Don't forget the surprise pieces. Then you are ready to begin.

Now, if there is one procedure I am emphatic about, it is trying to cut strips on the lengthwise grain. However, sometimes that doesn't make sense. Then the easier and more logical way to proceed is to cut a 1½-inch strip from one end of a 45-inch-wide piece of fabric, then cut it in half for the first two strips. It is easy to get fifty strips this way if you have twenty-five fabrics you want to use, as we did. If you only have twelve fabrics, cut two 1½-inch strips and you'll get four of each fabric chosen. If you are using some number in between, cut one full strip from some colors and two from others until you have the fifty half strips you need.

In fact, you only need thirty-six strips to make the patchwork squares (but no mistakes are allowed). I prefer to cut extra strips while the fabrics are out. They serve as a very inexpensive safety net. If I don't like some of the blocks achieved with a random arrangement, I can easily piece a few more strips. I can also sew strips together to make the satchel handles, a pocket, or whatever. If I don't want to use the extra strips, I just put them in a shoe box or basket where I store 1½-inch strips for a scrap-happy rainy day!

Piecing the Strips and Cutting the Triangles

1. Seam together, in random order, three sets of twelve strips. Because we chose to use parallel strips of consistent width, it was

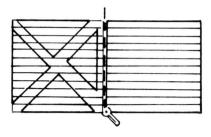

Figure 2

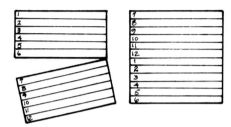

Figure 3

Figure 4

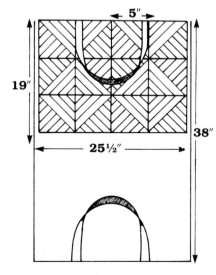

Figure 5

necessary to have half of the triangles positioned on an unseamed edge. That is why we needed to sew these strips together into sets of twelve.

2. Cut twenty-four triangles as shown (Figure 2). Be careful to offset the triangles so that the pattern of fabric strips will be different. We chose to add even more variety to the strip arrangements by cutting the pieced strip in half. We picked out the seam in the middle of the remaining half and rejoined the strips, seaming the top to the bottom (Figure 3) before cutting the next four triangles. This gives your blocks greater variety and visual appeal.

Making the Front

1. Seam triangles together to make twelve squares (Figure 4).

2. Seam together the twelve squares as shown in Figure 1, or in any pattern that pleases you. Once the squares are all joined together and pressed, they should measure at least 19 by 25 inches. If they don't, add a little border, as we did.

3. If they come out at least 19 by 25 inches, use the joined squares as a pattern to cut a piece that will become the back of the satchel. Seam together at the bottom. This will be the outside front and back of the satchel.

4. Use this new piece as a pattern to cut a lining and the fleece.

5. Place the fleece on the wrong side of the pieced rectangle and pin in place. Quilt through patchwork and fleece.

6. You may wish to put pockets in your satchel to hold your rotary cutter, patterns, marking pencils, pins, or just odds and ends. If so, you must make the pockets and attach to the lining at this point.

Straps

1. Cut two strips each, 1¾ by 25 inches long, from two different fabrics. (We lined the straps with contrasting fabrics.) Also cut two strips from fleece.

2. With the two fabric strips right sides together, place the fleece on top and sew ¼-inch seams down both long sides of the straps. Turn and press.

Finishing the Satchel

1. Position and pin straps into place on the quilted piece as shown in Figure 5.

2. Place the lining on top of the quilted piece, keeping right sides together, and seam at both ends as shown in Figure 6.

3. Now pull the lining and the quilted top apart from each other, until the two seams you just finished sewing line up one atop the other.

4. Using the diagram as a guide, sew the two long edges of the satchel together, making sure to leave an opening on one side to pull the satchel through (Figure 7).

5. Turn the satchel to the right side by pulling through the opening in the seam. Close the turning hole by hand or machine. Tuck the lining into the satchel and press.

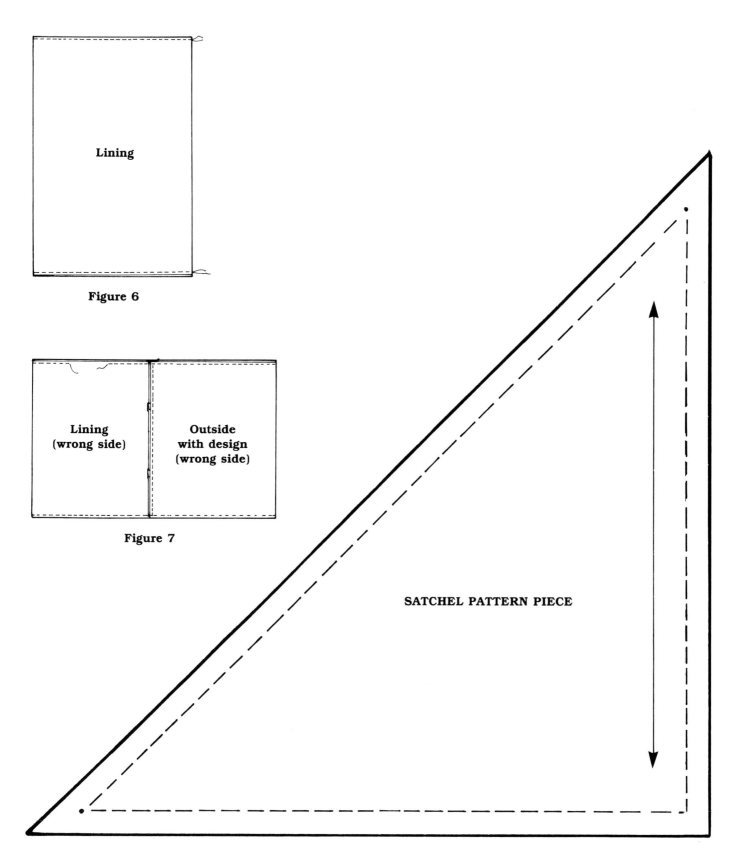

Lining

Figure 6

Lining
(wrong side)

Outside
with design
(wrong side)

Figure 7

SATCHEL PATTERN PIECE

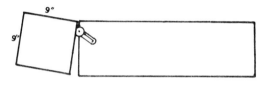

Figure 1: Victorian Shadows

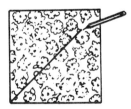

Figure 2

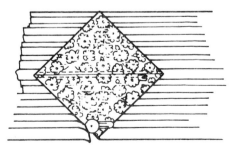

Figure 3

Victorian Shadows

APPROXIMATE SIZE:
   51½ × 51½ inches
MATERIALS NEEDED:
   Thirty assorted quarter-yard pieces
   ⅛ to ⅜ yard for border fabric

This quilt skillfully incorporates fabric that is string-pieced without a base (Figure 1). Many of the fabrics used for the strips are also used in the unpieced triangles to complete the scrap look. The black print fabric in the border was the controlling fabric for this quilt. Using darker colors in all the fabrics in the quilt made the colors in the black print stand out from the black background; the other fabrics were selected to complement those colors.

Making Pieced Fabric

About thirty different fabrics were used in this quilt. All were cut and pieced to make the yardage for the pieced triangles. Seventeen fabrics were used for the unpieced triangles. Starting with a quarter-yard piece, cut a 9-inch square from one end (Figure 2). Cut parallel but random-width strips, anywhere from 1 to 2 inches wide, from the rest. (Don't cut many 2-inch strips.)

Sew the strips of fabric together in random order. Make sure you vary the colors. Then press the string-pieced fabrics carefully. Keep strips straight . . . I repeat, *keep strips straight* while pressing. In effect, what you are doing is sewing striped fabric. The stripes must be parallel. While all the strips can be sewn together into one full piece, they can also be sewn together in smaller sections. Two or three smaller lengths will be easier to handle, and the scraps can be sewn together if necessary.

Sew-Before-You-Cut Triangles/Squares

This method is an adaptation of the Perfect-Pieced Triangles shown on pages 111 to 112. You can cut each triangle separately, as for the Rotary Mat Satchel, but I think you will like this method. You can only use this method easily with random-width strips. (No pattern. If you want to cut individually, draft an 8½-inch square and cut in half diagonally.)

1. Mark an 8½-inch square on the back of each of your 9-inch squares, and draw a diagonal line to make two triangles (Figure 3).
2. Place the square on the pieced fabric, right sides together, with the diagonal line parallel to the seams (Figure 4).
3. Stitch ¼ inch away from the diagonal line on both sides of the line. If your presser foot is not an accurate ¼ inch, you may want to mark the seam allowance and then stitch on the marked seam line. These seam lines do need to be straight or the square will not lie flat.
4. Now, using your markings as a guide, cut both layers of fabric along the 8½-inch square. Cut on the diagonal line between the stitching and open to find two pieced triangles. Press seams toward

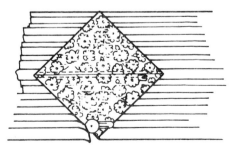

Figure 4

the unpieced triangle. There may be some very narrow strips of fabric, but that is not a problem. Save the extra pieced fabric to make the pieced border.

Finishing the Quilt

1. Arrange squares and piece desired design together.

2. Add borders. As with all borders, they should enhance *your* quilt, not fit our dimensions, so they may vary in width and quantity when you make your quilt. (Our borders are 1 inch and 2½ inches.) Layer, quilt, and bind. Our binding is ⅜ inch finished. (See Chapter 11 for details.)

Border Outlet Strips

These are a perfect solution for what to do when the fabric for the border has to be pieced and you don't want the seam to show. Add border outlets that look like they were planned.

The Antique String-Pieced Eight-Pointed Star

Circa 1890—probably from Pennsylvania

FINISHED SIZE:
   81 inches square

MATERIALS NEEDED FOR QUILT TOP:
   Equivalent of 4¾ yards of scraps (at least ¼ should be 9 inches long)
   2¾ yards of background fabric; 3½ yards for larger quilt
   Freezer or tracing paper
   Acrylic ruler, rotary cutter, and mat

This is the very first antique quilt I ever bought. At the time, I didn't think of scrap quilts as a category of quilts, but I knew I loved this quilt. The dark brown background fabric is the main controlling factor. For the method of construction given in this book, I recommend you use a nondirectional, small, textured print for the background fabric so that the seams added to simplify the construction will not be obvious.

The finished quilt (Figure 1), with nine 27-inch square stars, is approximately 81 inches square. This size would make a lovely large wall hanging or could be placed on a bed below the pillows.

The antique quilt pictured (page 40) uses whole pieces with no seams in the center squares. Cutting instructions are included should you choose to assemble the quilt in this whole-piecing manner. To simplify the assembly, however, we highly recommend the individually pieced star units (Figure 2), and have provided directions for them. Because the majority of the quilt surface is pieced from scraps, approximately 4⅔ yards of scraps will be needed. When selecting fabrics to create the quilt as pictured, at least one-fourth of the scraps must be a minimum of 9 inches long.

An optional extra row of stars makes a quilt approximately 81 by 108 inches, which is better suited for more complete coverage on a bed and even allows for a pillow tuck (Figure 3).

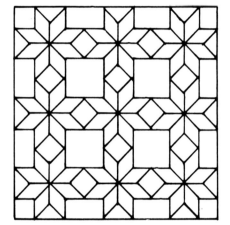

Figure 1: Antique String-Pieced Eight-Pointed Star

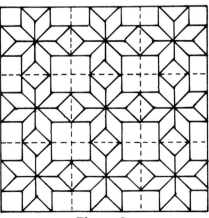

Figure 2

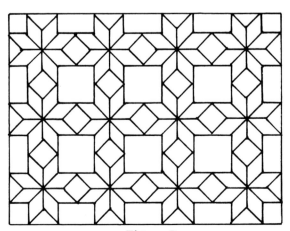

Figure 3

Making the String-Pieced Diamonds

1. Use the pattern piece provided. Make the actual pattern by tracing twice, joining the two pieces at the short line marked with the three diamonds. *Be very accurate.* Trace the diamond pattern onto the uncoated side of the freezer paper. Mark and cut seventy-two paper diamonds (ninety-six if opting for a larger quilt). These will be used as foundations for the string quilting. On each paper diamond, mark the horizontal sewing line at each tip (see pattern).

2. Use the 9-inch-long cut strips to cover the middle section of the diamond from one horizontal sewing line to the other. Referring to the information on string piecing (pages 29 to 30), cover the central area of each diamond. Start at the middle and work out, or start on one side and work across (Figure 4). Remember, variety is important for interest. Continue to add strips until the middle section of the paper diamond is covered (Figure 5). Make sure the strips overlap the horizontal sewing lines at both ends of the diamond. Depending on the width of the strips, some diamonds will have four strips, some five, and so on.

3. From your other pile of scraps, select a piece approximately 4 inches square (or make a pieced unit of that size). Lay the square on top of the string-piecing at one end of the diamond, with right sides together, and machine-stitch along the horizontal sewing line. Repeat to cover the opposite diamond tip.

4. Using your rotary cutter, mat, and acrylic ruler, trim the excess fabric away, *leaving a ¼-inch seam allowance on all sides* of the paper diamond.

5. In this manner, make seventy-two (ninety-six) string-quilted diamonds.

OPTIONS: Figure 6 shows two variations of string-piecing the diamond that would create a more refined pattern within the star.

Cutting the Background Fabric

1. Cut the following pieces. (The numbers in parentheses are the pieces needed to complete the larger version of the quilt.)

WHOLE-PIECING METHOD	INDIVIDUAL PIECING METHOD
4 (6) 16½-inch squares	36 (48) 8½-inch squares
8 (10) pieces 8½ × 16½	9 (12) 12¾-inch squares*
16 (21) 8½-inch squares	
3 (4) 12¾-inch squares*	

*Cut these squares into quarters diagonally to obtain right angle triangles (Figure 7).

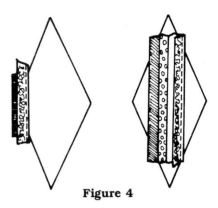

Figure 4

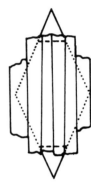

Figure 5

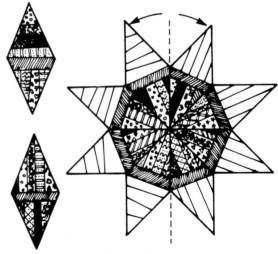

Figure 6

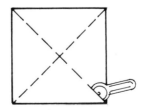

Figure 7

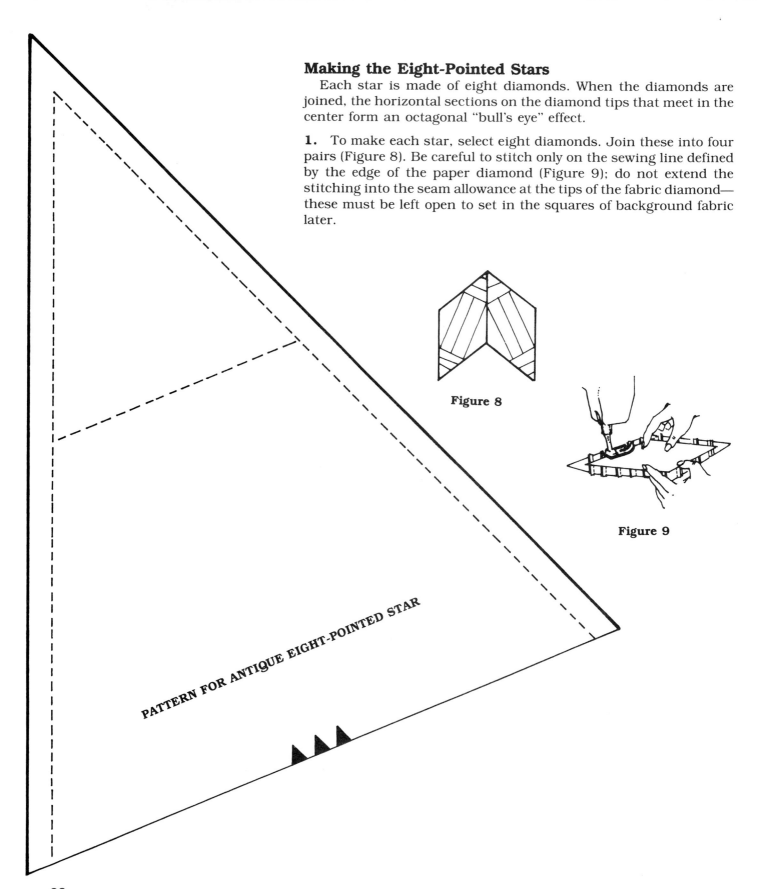

Making the Eight-Pointed Stars

Each star is made of eight diamonds. When the diamonds are joined, the horizontal sections on the diamond tips that meet in the center form an octagonal "bull's eye" effect.

1. To make each star, select eight diamonds. Join these into four pairs (Figure 8). Be careful to stitch only on the sewing line defined by the edge of the paper diamond (Figure 9); do not extend the stitching into the seam allowance at the tips of the fabric diamond— these must be left open to set in the squares of background fabric later.

Figure 8

Figure 9

PATTERN FOR ANTIQUE EIGHT-POINTED STAR

2. While diamonds are in pairs, insert the squares as illustrated (Figure 10). Pin each square along one side of the diamond edge, with right sides together. Match corners and stitching lines. Being careful to sew only on the stitching line by following the freezer paper, sew the seam from the outside edge of the diamond to the inner corner. Stop stitching two or three stitches before the inner corner seam allowance (Figure 11).

3. Press this seam away from the diamond.

4. Again, carefully matching corners and stitching lines right sides together, sew the second seam from the inside corner to the outside edge. Start stitching two or three stitches away from the inside corner. Although this will leave a very small hole in the corner between the diamonds and the square, the hole will not be visible when the seams are pressed, and leaving this hole will make the seams lie much more smoothly. When the seams are pressed as instructed, no batting will be able to work through these small holes in the finished quilt (Figure 12). Press this seam away from the diamond.

5. Sew pairs of diamonds together to create star halves (Figure 13); join the halves. Following the above instructions, insert one triangular piece in each half. Then join halves and insert remaining triangles. Press the seam allowances to one side so that they fan around the center of the star (Figure 14).

Assembling the Quilt Top

1. Following the instructions given above, make nine (twelve) stars. Leave the paper diamonds in place until the quilt top is complete.

2. Join the star sections in three (four) horizontal rows of three stars each. Then join these rows together.

3. Now you can safely remove the paper diamonds with your fingernail or the point of a seam ripper. Lift the tip of each paper diamond and gently tear the paper at the horizontal seam line.

Quilting and Finishing

Layer, quilt, and bind with separate ½-inch finished binding. See Chapter 11 for details.

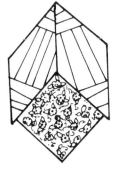

Figure 10

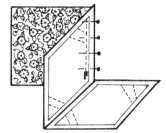

Figure 11

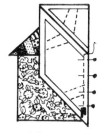

Figure 12

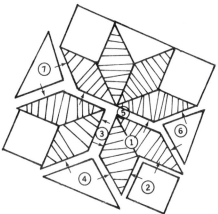

Figure 13

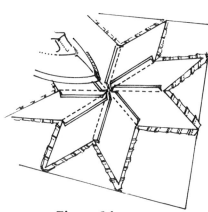

Figure 14

Single Eight-Pointed Star

APPROXIMATE SIZE:
  31 × 31 inches

MATERIALS NEEDED:
  ½-yard or larger scraps for background
  ⅛ to ¼-yard pieces for borders and bindings
  Selected scraps (ours used forty-one different fabrics)

One of the things that makes scrap quilts effective is the interplay of the many different fabrics. The same thing often makes small scrap patchwork items look strange. The eight-pointed star is an example of a small project that can be very effective because it has multiple units where the interplay can take place and yet has enough background area to be settling (Figure 1). The choice of the nondirectional, small-textured background print was important to provide that quiet setting for the many fabrics used in the star. The fabrics were selected not to try to duplicate the antique quilt, but to show that you can very easily get an antique look by careful fabric selection, making the new quilt compatible with the antique quilt, should you want to use them in the same room.

The size, shape, and directional placing of the scraps on the diamonds are determined in much the same way as for a single unit of the Antique Eight-Pointed Star Quilt. Our quilt was layered with about 4 inches of batting and backing extending all around to give plenty of opportunity to decide on borders.

The quilting pattern used emphasizes the shape of the star, and was quickly completed on the sewing machine. After the diamonds were quilted in the ditch, the background was quilted in lines, 1 inch apart, that echoed the shape of the star. After the interior part of the quilt was quilted, the borders were added using the Quilt-As-You-Sew technique. The border widths from the inside out are ½ inch and 1 inch finished. The binding is a finished ½ inch. (See Chapter 11 for more finishing details.)

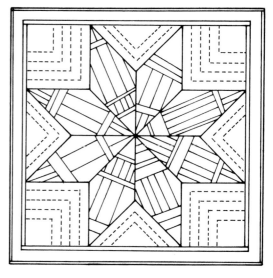

Figure 1: Single Eight-Pointed Star

NEVER throw away string-pieced fabric scraps. They make wonderful heart sachets or pin cushions. Sew them together again and get a piece of fabric big enough to make a teddy bear.

Nancy's Wastebasket Version

APPROXIMATE SIZE:
  52½ × 52½ inches

MATERIALS NEEDED:
  1 yard neutral background
  ⅝ yard contrasting border and binding
  Lots (2½ to 3½ yards) of scraps

Earlier in this book I mentioned Nancy Granner, a quilter I know who will only use real scraps for her scrap quilts. The quilt shown here (Figure 1) was made from strips her guild members threw away after an all-day seminar on strip piecing. We estimated that close to 400 different fabrics may have been used in this quilt. The key point to remember, though, is not that you must use 400 different fabrics, but that you can, and that they can be bright and muted, wild and crazy! Nancy's combined resourcefulness in acquiring and courage in putting together so many different fabrics resulted in a beautiful quilt. This is a perfect example of how scrap quilts can stretch your color palette. I admit it, there are some colors next to each other in this quilt that would have made me flinch, but Nancy had the courage to go ahead and put them together, and the end result is fabulous.

Knowing that I wanted to share the antique String-Quilted Eight-Pointed Star Quilt, you can imagine my excitement at being able to share this version made almost exactly 100 years later. It certainly is a tribute to the pleasing classic arrangement and technique.

Nancy's quilt is made with diamonds exactly half the size of those in the Antique String-Pieced Eight-Pointed Star. The quilt was made by the individually pieced star method. Following the directions for that quilt, the squares would be cut 4½ inches and the squares for cutting the triangles would be 7 inches. The red border strips are 1½ inches wide and the pieced border is 4½ inches.

Nancy was also creative in her use of numerous sizes and shapes of fabric strips. The widths of the fabrics range from 1½ inches to barely ¼ inch. The scraps are pieced at random, with varying shapes and sizes fitting together in many directions. The only consistency is the finished shape of the diamond and the width of the border. There is a general tendency for the strips to go across the diamonds and for the border strips to be perpendicular to the edge of the quilt, but it is only a general tendency.

The background fabric is a perfect example of how a nondirectional, small textured print will hide seam lines. Even more important, it is that same fabric that helps give continuity or relief to an otherwise very busy quilt. A 1-inch red border and matching binding are also design features important to controlling the quilt.

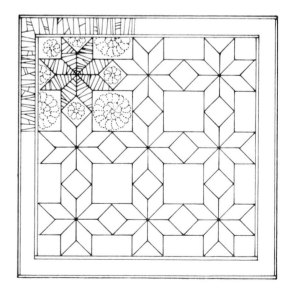

Figure 1: Nancy's Wastebasket Version

Finishing the Quilt

The floral quilting on the background fabric adds interest and also contributes to disguising seam lines. The diamonds are quilted just inside their edges, and the border is edge-quilted on individual scraps approximately every 1 to 2 inches. The hand quilting was done by Nancy, her mother, and her father's cousin—the latter two both octogenarians! The binding is ½ inch finished. (See Chapter 11 for details.)

QUILTING PATTERN FOR SMALL BLOCK

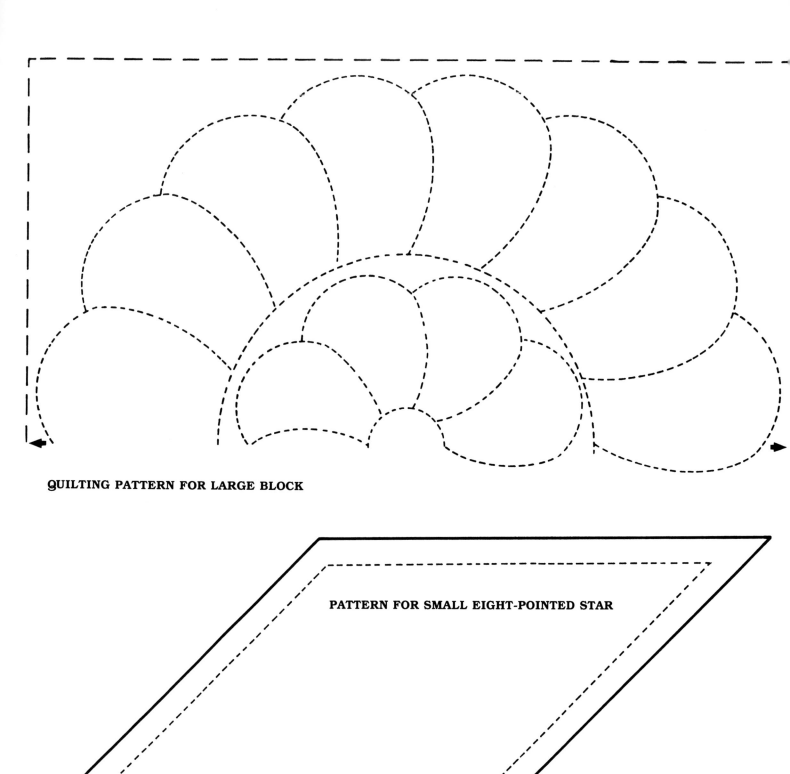

QUILTING PATTERN FOR LARGE BLOCK

PATTERN FOR SMALL EIGHT-POINTED STAR

One-Patch Quilts

There are many quilts that require only one pattern piece. They lend themselves particularly to scrap quilts, because no repetition of color or fabric is necessary to create a patchwork pattern. We call the special kind of quilts where every piece is a different fabric charm quilts. Charm quilts are usually one-patch quilts, but not always.

It would be easy to do an entire book on one-piece scrap quilts. Instead, here are some idea-stimulating diagrams of common one-patch shapes—and directions for quilts made from two classic shapes.

A THOUSAND PYRAMIDS

This is one of my favorite one-patch quilts (Figure 1). It is made from half of a 45-degree diamond. Usually the dark triangles point up and the light ones down. Be sure to put some medium colors in both the light and dark sections to keep it interesting.

RIGHT-ANGLE TRIANGLES

A very versatile shape. Here are two patterns (Figure 2) that use only light and dark right-angle triangles, the perfect vehicle for scrap quilts. Do you see the subunits? One could easily be worked in sets of four squares and one in nine. (See Perfect-Pieced Triangles, page 111, for an easy way to make lots of these two triangle squares.)

HEXAGONS

Hexagons (Figure 3) have fascinated hand piecers for years. They are often put together in subunits like the flower or the diamond, with final assembly done later. For a nice machine-piecing method, see the directions given in Chapter 7, where the hexagon is used as a border on a Log Cabin quilt (page 79).

60-DEGREE DIAMONDS

The close relationship between 60-degree diamonds and hexagons (three diamonds make one hexagon—Figure 4) makes them equally fascinating and exciting to play with.

Figure 1

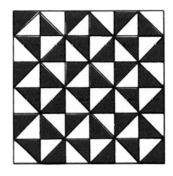 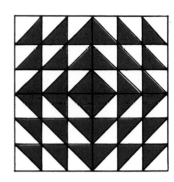

Figure 2

 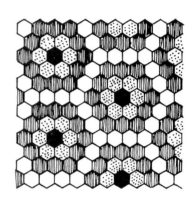

Figure 3

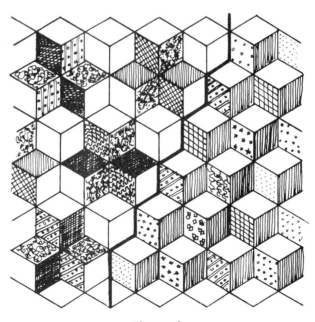

Figure 4

Double Hammerhead

Circa 1900—1915

APPROXIMATE SIZE:
   87 × 81 inches
MATERIALS NEEDED FOR QUILT TOP:
   380 scraps at least 5½ × 6 inches
   Template material

A very common way to fabricate one-patch quilts is to use a simple light/dark alternating pattern. The full-size Double Hammerhead in our photo is a good example of this.

There are several other names for this quilt, including a couple we created for this book.

Making the Hammerhead Patterns, Marking and Cutting

1. Use the large Hammerhead pattern (page 50) and make the actual pattern by tracing the cutting size onto a stiff material (preferably cuttable acrylic or plastic). It is probably worth the effort to cut another piece the exact finished size so that you can mark both the cutting and sewing lines.
2. Cut 380 "charms" from 380 fabrics, or cut 380 assorted pieces. Mark and cut individually or stack several pieces and use the rotary cutter and mat if your pattern is permanent enough. Then go back and mark the sewing line. Snip at the center mark on all sides of the shape. Every half inch, clip the concave sides perpendicular to the seam line, and within a couple threads of the stitching line. (Concave is the side that dips in or "caves in" toward the center.)

Piecing the Quilt Top

1. Laying two pieces right sides together, and alternating vertically and horizontally, match center notches and outside edges. Pin in place (Figure 1). It seems easier to have the convex curve on the bottom, and to stretch the concave curve to fit when you are pinning. It is also easier to sew the pieces with the concave curve on top. That is a luxury you have when you are piecing the single rows. Press seams toward one side, but alternate their direction so that they will not overlap when the rows are put together (Figure 2). Continue, making rows of twenty.
2. After sewing nineteen rows of twenty pieces (or you may wish to work with shorter rows, especially to begin with), begin to join the rows together. Match centers and seams, pin in place right sides together, and stitch. It's a little awkward to shift back and forth and reposition at the machine, but if speed is your desire, machine piecing is worth it.

Hand piecers often like to stitch these in sets of four (Figure 3), then piece those together in sets of four, and so on, to keep the units smaller.

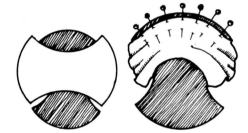

Figure 1

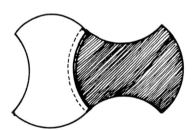

Figure 2

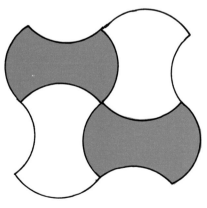

Figure 3

Finishing the Quilt

Layer, quilt, and bind with separate ½-inch binding all around. Because of the curved edges, bias binding is recommended. This would also be a perfect quilt to consider tying instead of quilting (see Chapter 11 for details).

There is a method of layering the quilt top with batting and backing. Just as with a pillow top, stitch around the outside edge and then turn inside out. That would be a time saver on this quilt. After clipping, turning, and pressing, quilt ½ inch from the edge all around.

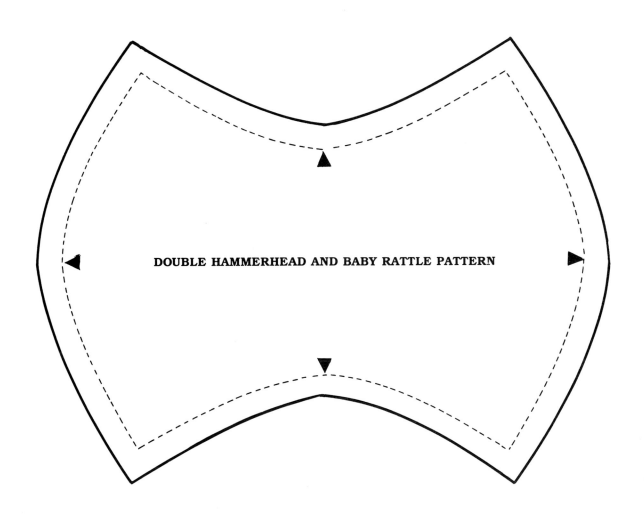

DOUBLE HAMMERHEAD AND BABY RATTLE PATTERN

Baby Rattle

APPROXIMATE SIZE:
  33 × 41 inches
  Plus 2½-inch ruffle all around

MATERIALS NEEDED:
  Pink and blue scraps for forty-two 5½-inch by 6-inch pieces
  ¾ yard background fabric
  ⅞ yard ruffle fabric
  Crib-size precut batting
  1 yard backing fabric
  1 yard each of ⅛-inch pink ribbon and blue ribbon

Double Hammerhead is just not an appropriate name for a baby quilt. Since the shape also looks like a rattle, we chose this name. Using the same size pattern as the Double Hammerhead, but only sixty-three pieces, these collected pink and blue fabrics were turned into a darling crib quilt (Figure 1).

Cutting

To make the arrangement shown, cut twenty-two blue pieces; twenty pink; and twenty-one matching pieces of background fabric.

Piecing the Quilt Top

1. Referring to the Double Hammerhead directions, prepare fabrics for piecing as before. Piece two rows of nine alternating pink and blue fabrics; two rows of five alternating pink and blue; and four rows of three alternating pink and blue. Piece two rows of seven and two rows of three pieces from the background fabric. Piece one row of three pieces, with the center piece background fabric, and the two outer pieces from blue.

You can create a new pattern that eliminates seams, instead of piecing matching fabric, but I like it better with seams, especially when you want to machine-quilt "in the ditch"—you won't have a ditch without the seams.

2. Refer to the illustration to make sure you are positioning horizontal and vertical pieces correctly according to color (see Figure 1 for Double Hammerhead Quilt, page 48).

Figure 1

Finishing the Quilt

1. Stay-stitch just less than ¼ inch from the outside of the quilt all around. Press under the seam allowance, clipping as necessary. Cut two strips of background fabric 4½ inches wide and the length of the quilt top. Pin the pressed sides in place with an equal amount of strip exposed. Appliqué in position.

2. Repeat for the ends. Make mock mitered corner.

3. Layer and quilt as desired, leaving edges free. (See Chapter 11 for details.)

4. To make the ruffle, cut five strips of fabric 5½ by 45 inches (approximately 325 inches). Seam ends together to make a circle. Fold in half, wrong sides together, and press. Gather to fit quilt (approximately 148 inches). Stitch to right side of the top of the quilt, with raw edges even. Catch batting in the seams. Open out so that the ruffle is in correct position and seam allowances face in. Trim away excess batting and seam allowances.

5. Turn under the backing and stitch it shut by hand, making sure to catch the seam allowance of the ruffle.

6. Make six bows from each ribbon and stitch securely on alternate background blocks.

Mini-Spools Wall Quilt

APPROXIMATE SIZE:
   15 × 19 inches

MATERIALS NEEDED:
   Little scraps

The Mini-Spools miniature wall hanging was made with exactly the same number of pieces as the crib quilt, but with a much smaller pattern piece. It was hand-pieced.

Cutting

Cut thirty-three pieces from darker colors, and thirty from lighter colors. Include some medium fabrics in each group. The Mini-Spools miniature quilt was laid out to give the impression of light coming through an opening. You will want to cut some extra pieces to play with so you get just the right gradations. These fabrics were easy to choose because they were the scraps left over from the Victorian Shadows Quilt shown on page 35. One of the darker colors has been repeated as a backing fabric in the pictured wall hanging.

Piecing the Top

1. Refer to the directions for the Double Hammerhead and Baby Rattle for the piecing methods to use.

2. Settle on the arrangement. Piece in horizontal rows. These pieces were actually identified with numbers on pieces of tape to prevent rearranging unintentionally while sewing.

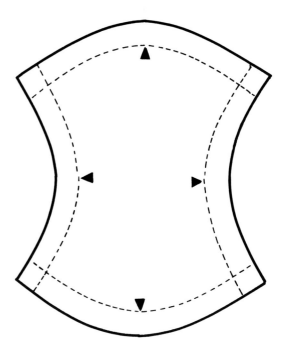

MINI-SPOOLS PATTERN

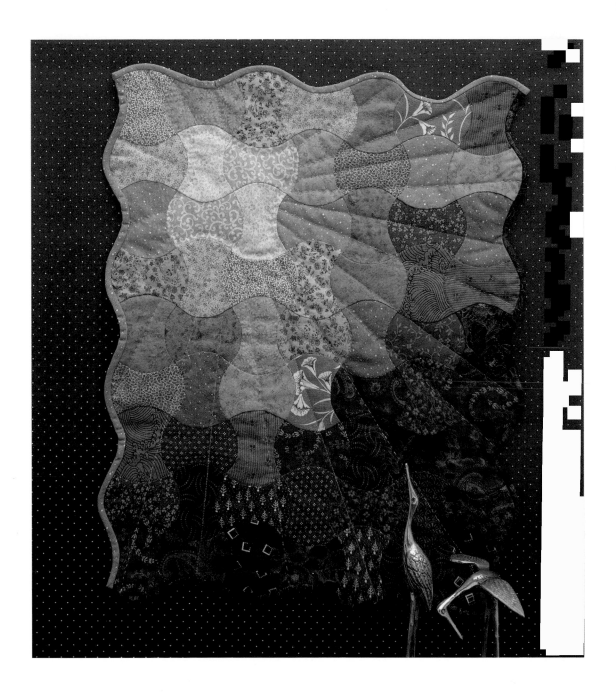

Finishing

Layer and quilt as desired. Because of the unique arrangement of color, the quilting lines were selected to accentuate the feeling of light radiating. All stitching lines radiate from the point where the four light fabrics meet. This quilt was hand-quilted with a thick metallic thread on every other radiating row of quilting and machine-quilted with metallic thread on the others. The curved edges are finished with bias binding. (See Chapter 11 for finishing details.)

Illusions

APPROXIMATE SIZE:
   30 inches square

MATERIALS NEEDED:
   Short, 1¾-inch-wide strips
   Or 261 squares of scraps 1¾ × 1¾ inch
   1 yard center strips and border fabric
   ⅛ yard contrasting fabric for narrow border

Using Squares Only

This method (Figure 1) is not appropriate if you want to do any directional quilting in the band between the center and corner units, as the seams are too distracting. The quilt photographed was made using the optional method explained on the next page. This, however, is really a simpler construction method.

The design is completely developed in grid form (no patterns necessary), with nineteen squares in each direction. You will need the equivalent of 185 1¾-inch squares of medium and dark scraps. You will need 56 matching and contrasting squares for the diagonal outline and 120 light matching or scrap squares. Arrange squares of fabric to develop the design. Piece together as diagramed. Use as many quick-piecing techniques as possible, or cut squares and stitch them together one at a time.

There are four squares of matching fabric in every horizontal row of fabric on both sides of the center square. You may prefer using assorted light fabrics to make the quilt look more interesting.

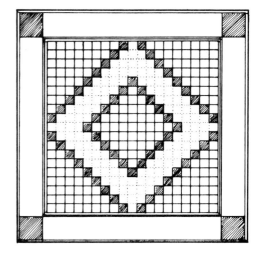

Figure 1

To Make a King-Size Quilt

Here's a great idea for an easy, dramatic king-size quilt. Start with a grid measuring 23 squares wide by 23 squares high (Figure 2). Cut 4-inch squares, add a 10-inch border all around. You will need 261 medium and dark squares, 64 matching, contrasting squares, and 120 light squares, plus 3 yards of border fabric.

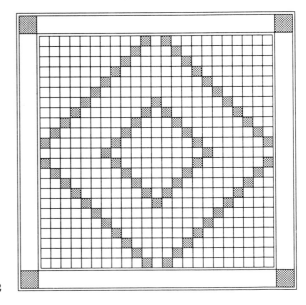

Figure 2

Figure 3

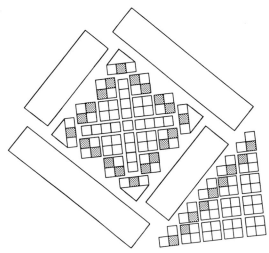

Figure 4

Optional Method—Using the Center Strip Method

This method (Figure 3) was chosen to eliminate seam lines, as one fabric was going to be used throughout the entire center area.

1. Piece the center section as diagramed (Figure 4). Use quick-piecing techniques (see Chapter 7) or lay out all squares and stitch together one by one. The illustration shows four-patch units being used in preliminary piecing.

2. The last square in every row should be a fabric to match the wide diagonal strips. The edges of these squares will extend beyond the next seam and be trimmed off later (Figure 5). Setting triangles could be substituted for these squares, but because each is so small and will be sewn to a straight edge, the risk of extra stretch from the bias seam is minimal. (For more detail on setting triangles, see the Pink Mosaic Crib Quilt, page 59.)

3. Use the same contrasting fabric in the next to last square of each row to outline the interior section.

4. Add 4-inch-wide strips as illustrated (Figure 5). Measure the center square for the exact length of these strips.

5. Figure 6 shows both the back and front after all four strips have been added.

Making and Adding Corner Sections

1. Make four corner sections as illustrated in Figure 4, using contrasting squares and squares cut from diagonal strip fabric, as in the center section.

2. Add corner sections one at a time by laying the corner unit right side down on the center and perfectly matching the outside corner square of the unit and the center square of the center. Remember seam allowances. The outside corner square should actually extend ¼ inch beyond the center square on two sides, and the other two sides should line up (Figure 7).

The outside edge will be jagged. Trim this away *after* successfully adding all four sides—"just in case." I find that drawing a straight line to connect the stitched corners of the contrasting squares makes the stitching line more accurate.

3. Proceed around the center square, adding each corner in the same way. As each successive corner unit is positioned, the first square on one unit will overlap the last square on the other, and should line up just as accurately as the center square.

4. After all corner units are in place, pressed and completed, check to be sure center square is square, then trim away excess points and edges of strips.

Adding Borders and Finishing

This quilt features a narrow flap border, a second narrow border (⅝ inch) and a final 3¼-inch border with contrasting corner squares. The ⅜-inch separate binding matches the last border. (See Chapter 11 for details on making the flap, layering, quilting, and binding.)

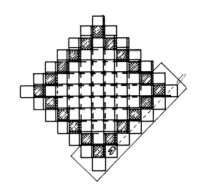

Figure 5

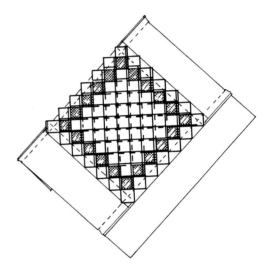

Figure 6 (back)

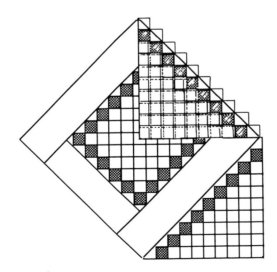

Figure 7

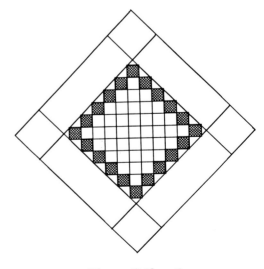

Figure 6 (front)

CHAPTER 7

Strip-Piecing Techniques

It is easier to teach strip techniques in a class than to describe them in a book, but as I have an opportunity to share with so many more people in this book than I could ever teach in person, I must write out the instructions. From an author's point of view, describing old-style piecing one block at a time is much easier than writing out the instructions for strip techniques. For example, the next quilt and its several pages of instruction could be replaced with patterns for three squares (see Figure 1) and instructions to cut and piece as shown.

I really believe that if more people understood strip techniques, they would have more fun making quilts and be more productive at the same time.

Strip-piecing techniques work when two or more fabrics are repeatedly positioned side by side. It entails cutting strips as wide as the desired square (*finished* size plus two ¼-inch seam allowances) and sewing them together in rows in the same order as they appear. Then, by cutting across the sewn and pressed strips in increments the same as the width of the original strips, you end up with pre-pieced squares. This method not only saves time; the real bonus is that it is both easier and more accurate for most sewers.

If you want to make more quilts in the same amount of time required for finishing a quilt one block at a time, strip-piecing techniques are worth learning. You do have to think ahead, but it isn't hard thinking, once you have done it a time or two.

It would be easy to think you can't use strip-piecing techniques to advantage when making a scrap quilt. But think again: The quilts in this chapter are *all* made with scraps and start with strips.

Quilt designs that emphasize squares and strips are most conducive to strip-piecing methods. In antique quilts of this type (Figure 1), the little squares of each four-patch block were cut individually and sewn together one by one. If you prefer to make the Pink Mosaic Crib Quilt traditionally, simply cut the scrap fabrics into 1½-inch squares and assemble the blocks accordingly.

I can't say enough positive things about rotary cutters and strip-piecing techniques. If you aren't using a rotary cutting system and didn't read the information on page 20, please refer to it before you start projects in this chapter. While strips can be marked with a pencil and ruler and cut with scissors, the rotary cutting system is ideal for projects that benefit from strip-piecing techniques.

Figure 1: Pink Mosaic Crib Quilt

Pink Mosaic Crib Quilt

APPROXIMATE SIZE:
    35 × 40¼ inches
MATERIALS REQUIRED:
    1¼ yards of pink print background fabric
    ¾ yard of muslin (includes binding)
    Scraps of pink fabric totaling ¼ yard
    Or one 1½ × 42-inch strip of six different fabrics
    1⅛ yards of backing fabric
    Precut crib-size batting

Making the Four-Patch Units

Each finished block is only 4 inches square.

1. Cut six 1½ by 42-inch strips of muslin. Cut each strip in half to be 21 inches long.

2. Cut twelve 1½-inch-wide strips from at least four or five different pink fabrics. Each strip should be approximately 20 inches long. If you are working with smaller scraps, you'll need more strips. To be most efficient, keep each fabric together as you work.

3. Using a ¼-inch seam allowance, sew the pink and muslin strips together (Figure 2). You should have plenty of muslin to accommodate different lengths of pink strips. Press all seam allowances toward the pink fabric.

4. Place one pair of pieced strips on top of another, with right sides of opposite fabrics together and one end matching (Figure 3). Carefully align the seams. When the fabrics are positioned as shown, the seam allowances are pressed in opposite directions, serving as "automatic pins" that help you align the seam lines.

5. Cut across the pair of layered strip sets in 1½-inch-wide segments. The rotary cutter is the ideal tool because it cuts through the fabric while it is lying perfectly flat, eliminating the risk of distortion. Cut a total of 84 stacked pairs or 168 two-square units. The stacked pairs (with matching pink fabric sections) are already correctly positioned to take to the sewing machine and chain-piece.

6. Stitch "prestacked pairs," keeping orientation of pink and muslin the same for all the blocks. If necessary to assemble pairs, select two cut units that have the same pink fabric (Figure 4), turning one unit upside down to position the fabrics correctly. Press the new seam allowance to one side. In this manner, make eighty-four four-patch units.

Making the Sixteen-Patch or Mosaic Blocks

The Mosaic or sixteen-patch blocks are made of four four-patch units sewn together. For each of the twelve blocks, choose four four-patch units that have the same pink fabric. Join these units into two pairs, then sew two of these units together to make a block (Figure 5). As seam allowances are already pressed in opposite directions, it should be easy to match the seam lines (Figure 6).

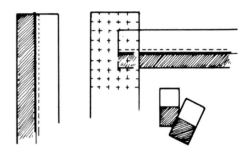

Figure 2   **Figure 3**

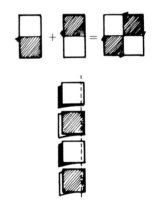

Figure 4

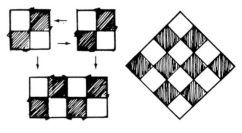

Figure 5   **Figure 6**

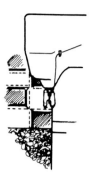

Figure 7

Figure 8

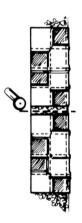

Figure 9

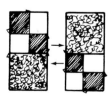

Figure 10

Making the Pieced Border Squares

Check the size of your four-patch units. They should be 2½ inches square. If they are slightly larger or smaller, it's fine as long as they are consistent. The quilt will finish slightly larger or smaller, but you will need to make minor adjustments as you proceed. (If your four-patch units are not 2½ inches, use the measurement of your patches instead of 2½ inches in the next steps.)

You may cut out 2½-inch background squares and sew them to the four-patch units one by one, but I prefer to sew the four patches to a long strip of 2½-inch-wide background fabric (Figure 7), and then cut across the strip to make blocks. This streamlined approach results in perfect-size squares because you use the four-patch as a template for the plain square.

Making the Four Corner Units

1. Select eight four-patch units for the corner squares. In our quilt, all eight units have the same pink fabric, but you may want the random look achieved with less planning. Sew the four-patch units in pairs, matching fabric squares in the center (Figure 8).

2. To begin the chain-piecing process, cut one strip of background fabric 2½ by 18 inches. Place a pieced corner unit right sides together with the background fabric strip and stitch them together along the length of the strip.

3. Place a second corner unit on the fabric directly against the bottom edge of the first one and continue to stitch (Figure 9). Sew all four corner units to the background fabric strip in this manner.

4. With a rotary cutter, cut through the background fabric between the pieced units. Before proceeding, square up the patches and the joined rectangles of background fabric. Using the lines on your acrylic ruler as a guide, trim any excess fabric from each side of the block. This enables you to match the background fabric piece precisely with the joined four-patch units.

5. When all four corner units are sewn and trimmed, press the joining seam allowances toward the nonpieced squares.

Making the Remaining Border Units

Cut four more 2½ by 18-inch strips of background fabric. Follow steps 2 through 4 to chain-piece the remaining four-patch units and cut out prepieced squares. Press the new seam allowances toward the nonpieced squares. Join these units in pairs (Figure 10) to complete fourteen pieced squares.

Joining the Pieced Units to the Alternate Squares

The same chain-piecing technique as that used on the corners will be used here to join the pieced blocks to strips of background fabric and then cut in presewn units. Measure your border squares and Mosaic blocks. They should measure 4½ inches square. (If your blocks are a different size, use that measurement instead of 4½ inches in the following instructions.)

1. Cut five 4½ by 20-inch strips of background fabric.

2. Use three of these strips to chain-piece the twelve Mosaic blocks.

Figure 11

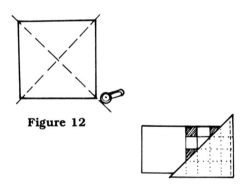

Figure 12

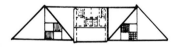

Figure 13

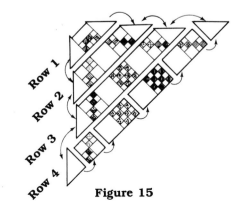

Figure 14

Figure 15

Use the two remaining strips to chain-piece one corner square and seven of the pieced border squares.

3. Trim out all twenty block/square units. Press all these seam allowances toward the nonpieced squares.

The Diagonal Set Layout

After chain-piecing the blocks and alternate squares, you can begin to lay out the diagonal rows that will make up the quilt. Arrange the blocks as diagramed (Figure 11). I use the floor, as that allows me to stand back and study the arrangement. To achieve an authentic scrap look, do not overplan the placement of your patches in terms of color or pattern.

Making the Setting Triangles

Diagonal set quilts are almost always more interesting than straight set. During the layout process, however, surprise triangular spaces are formed on the outside edges, and they need to be filled. Your first inclination may be to make the necessary triangular pieces by cutting a square in half diagonally. This would give you a triangle that would almost fit the space, but the outside (longest) edge of the new triangle would be on the bias. Because a bias edge stretches so easily, distortion is more likely to occur. Whenever possible, you want to avoid having outside edges of the quilt top be on the bias.

To eliminate the bias-edge problem and still have the correct size right-angle triangle, cut a 7½-inch square in half diagonally in both directions. That will create four right-angle triangles (Figure 12). As you need eighteen triangles to complete the rows, you will need to make five 7½-inch squares. Do the new triangles seem bigger than necessary? They are. That is because we want "floating" triangles. They will give an extra amount of background fabric before the first applied border.

Piecing the Diagonal Rows

1. The easiest way to piece the diagonal rows is to join the patch/ block combinations within each row first. Press seams toward nonpieced blocks. (Refer again to Figure 11.)

2. Next, sew the setting triangles in the appropriate spaces. Each diagonal row will begin and end with one of the setting triangles. (The four triangles that make up the four corners of the quilt will be added later.) Line up the right angle of the setting triangle with a corner of the patchwork block so that the hypotenuse (longest edge) will become the outside edge of the quilt. The tips of the triangles will extend beyond the patchwork in both directions (Figure 13). Stitch and press toward the triangles.

3. When the pieces within each diagonal row have been sewn together, the completed rows can be stitched together. Begin in the upper left corner with the single Mosaic block in Row 1 and, with right sides of fabric together and seams matching, sew it to Row 2 (Figure 14). Row 3 is then joined to Row 2, and so on until all the diagonal rows have been sewn together (Figure 15).

NOTE: When joining the rows, the extending tips of the triangles will be sewn one over the other, thus creating the effect of floating triangles. Trim off the stitched triangle tips on the back of the quilt, and trim away excess seam allowances before placing the quilt top over the batting and backing fabrics.

Doing the First Quilting

This quilt can be completely finished as a top and quilted traditionally, but it actually was finished using a Quilt-As-You-Sew method. (For more information see Chapter 8.)

1. Select a quilt backing and batting about 38 by 45 inches—that is, approximately 5 inches larger all the way around than the quilt interior. Layer the batting on the backing, right side down, and center the pressed top, right side up, on the batting. Baste the layers together or safety pin securely.
2. Following the seams of the 4½-inch squares, machine-quilt in the ditches created. The empty pink squares create a perfect place to run a simple row of hand quilting, if desired.

Adding the Borders and Corner Triangles

The setting triangles have created a space in the quilt that looks like a narrow border and matches the alternating squares. Because the four-patch blocks go diagonally across the corners, a simple 1-inch contrasting border could be added before background corners; that would accent the octagonal shape.

1. Add the corner strips for the narrow border first. To make the corner border strips, cut four muslin strips 1½ by 6 inches.
2. When sewing the strips to the quilt top, place right sides down on the quilt corner. Align each strip with the edge of the corner block (Figure 16). When stitching, you will be sewing through four layers—quilt border, quilt top, quilt batting, and quilt backing. After joining the border pieces, press the seam back very lightly and trim any excess fabric at the ends.
3. After the four short corner strips are complete, add the muslin borders (Figure 17). They are 1½ inches wide by the measured length of the quilt. Press each seam lightly and trim away any excess.
4. An unusual element of this quilt is the corner triangle design. These triangles are cut from the background fabric. You need two 4½-inch squares of background fabric. Cut each square in half diagonally to form the four corner triangles. With right sides together, sew the corner triangles to the muslin border and through all layers (Figure 18). Flip back and press in place to square the corners.
5. Cut four 2½ by 37-inch strips of background fabric for the outside borders. The side borders are attached in the same Quilt-As-You-Sew manner as the contrasting border pieces: first the sides, then the top and bottom, for a blunt corner finish.

Finishing

See Chapter 11 for information on making and applying a separate French-fold binding. Strips 2½ inches wide are allowed in the cutting diagram.

Figure 16

Figure 17

Figure 18

Full-Size Blue Mosaic

APPROXIMATE SIZE:
    78 × 98 inches

MATERIALS NEEDED:
    5¾ yards for background and binding
    1 yard for contrasting border blocks and flap
    Large variety of scraps

One of the tricks to relaxed quiltmaking is being comfortable with a technique. It is fun, once you know how to make a quilt, to make it again—especially when the mimicry is barely recognizable. Look at the diagram for this full-size quilt (Figure 1) and compare it to the Pink Mosaic Crib Quilt. They are just alike, **except** for:

- The arrangement of the Mosaic block. On the crib quilt, there are two colors, light and medium. On the full-size block, there are three fabrics. The orientation of the fabrics is also different (Figure 2).
- The cut strip for the crib quilt Mosaic is 1½ inches wide; for the full-size quilt it is 2½ inches wide.
- There are only twelve Mosaic blocks in the crib quilt; thirty-five are needed for the full-size quilt.
- The crib quilt has scraps, muslin, and background fabric in the border blocks. The border blocks on the full-size quilt were made with only two fabrics, the background fabric and a constant contrasting fabric. I had intended to use scrap blocks in the border, but decided the quilt was too busy and needed a controlling factor in the border.
- The large quilt doesn't have the contrasting narrow border around the blocks.
- The large quilt does have a flap tucked into the binding. (See Chapter 11 for instructions for making the flap.)

Otherwise, the two quilts are just alike!

Figure 1

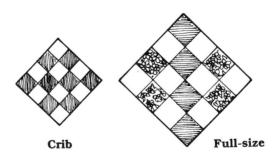

Crib   Full-size

Figure 2

Bonus Four-Patch Crib Quilt

APPROXIMATE SIZE:
   33½ × 38 inches

MATERIALS REQUIRED:
   1⅛ yards background fabric
   ¼ yard contrasting border and binding
   Scrap four-patch blocks

In the descriptive information about the Blue Mosaic Quilt, I mentioned that I had intended to use scrap four-patch blocks in the border, but did not. What do you suppose happened to those scrap blocks? You guessed it: They became this bonus quilt. Compare the diagram for the Bonus Four-Patch and that for the Pink Mosaic Crib Quilt (page 58).

Once again, they are just alike *except* we substituted a four-patch block for any block that had piecing. The direction that the dark half of the block goes alternates as you go across and down the quilt. As it happens, the size of the blocks is very similar, but if it weren't, you could simply adjust the size of the alternate blocks to match the size of the newly pieced block.

See how easy it is to keep disguising the same quilt?

P.S. There were still a few little four-patch units left; they got pieced into an abstract backing for this quilt.

Bonus Four-Patch Crib Quilt

Tennessee "Hard Times" Scrap Quilt

Circa 1900–1910—probably from Tennessee

APPROXIMATE SIZE:
   75 × 84 inches

MATERIALS NEEDED:
   3⅜ yards of navy prints
   1⅜ yards of yellow prints
   ⅝ yard of red print
   Scraps totaling approximately 3¼ yards

Because I purchased this quilt in Tennessee, I always just called it my Tennessee Scrap Quilt. The back is just as scrappy as the front, with seven different homespun-looking fabrics pieced and patched together. The quilt clearly says, "Use it up, or do without." Then I heard someone talk about a "hard times" quilt and I adopted that phrase for this quilt.

Some of the 1⅝-inch blocks in this quilt, which is also called "Cobblestones," are more organized than others in terms of color placement. Some have random fabric placement, others have each fabric consistently placed. Most, but not all of the blocks have a bright yellow accent fabric for the outer border of triangles. Light and dark contrast remains fairly constant.

If you choose to follow the more primitive pattern of the quilt photographed, you might want to make a few blocks consistently, as directed on page 71, then mix up your prepieced scrap units to make random blocks. You will probably want to follow through with mismatched navy fabrics in the solid blocks, not every block with a yellow accent, and the single block of printed patchwork in one corner.

Now, where do you think that came from? Since I personally always push my deadlines, I've always presumed that the maker of this top had friends coming over to help her quilt at a given time. She either miscalculated how many blocks she had or how much time it would take to put them together, so she put in one block of printed patchwork at the last minute. (Maybe she thought people would regard this as her humility block, except that with just one look you could quickly see enough other mistakes to satisfy that need.) Did you notice there are borders on just two sides? Who knows whether that was an omission due to lack of time or money, or just because the other two sides weren't really necessary.

"Not Such Hard Times" Scrap Quilt

APPROXIMATE SIZE:
   81 × 98 inches

MATERIALS NEEDED:
   3⅜ yards for alternating plain squares
   1⅜ yards sparkling accents around pieced blocks
   1 yard for first border
   1½ yards for second border
   Scraps totaling at least 3¼ yards but coordinated in each block

If you just can't bring yourself to re-create something as primitive as the "Hard Times" quilt, this design would interpret very nicely if all of the fabric squares in each block were consistent but all of the blocks used a different combination of fabrics. Go ahead and use a matching fabric in all the alternate squares and make the sparkling triangles consistent through the whole quilt. Add two borders, 3 and 5 inches, all around (second half of Figure 1).

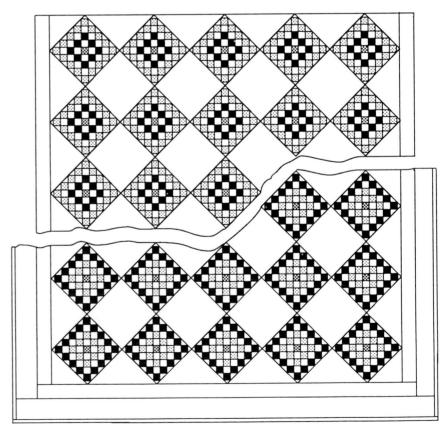

**Figure 1: Tennessee "Hard Times" (top)
"Not Such Hard Times" (bottom)**

Strip Piecing

1. Select three principal fabrics for the first block. These three fabrics can be strip-pieced into units to streamline the assembly of the block. The block breaks down into units as illustrated in Figure 1.

2. From the three fabrics selected for the block, cut strips 2 by 17 inches, 2 by 25 inches, and 2 by 32 inches (Figure 2). Sew these strips together as shown.

3. With a rotary cutter, cut segments 2 inches wide across the width of the strip set (Figure 2).

4. Cut five 2-inch squares from two different scrap fabrics.

5. For the yellow print setting triangles, cut ten 3½ by 42-inch strips. Cut twelve 3½-inch squares from each strip. Cut each square in quarters diagonally, cutting four triangles from each square. You will need sixteen of the small setting triangles for each block.

6. Sew one setting triangle onto the end of each row of pieced squares. Join the rows to assemble the block. Combine all of the prepieced units to join all the squares in diagonal rows as shown in Figure 1.

7. For the corner triangles, cut three 2 by 42-inch strips of yellow print fabric. From these, cut sixty 2-inch squares. Cut each square in half diagonally to obtain 120 corner triangles. Stitch one triangle onto each corner of the completed block.

8. Make twenty-nine blocks in this manner.

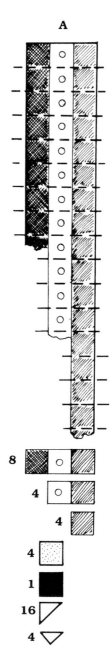

A

8

4

4

Plus: 4

1

16

4

B

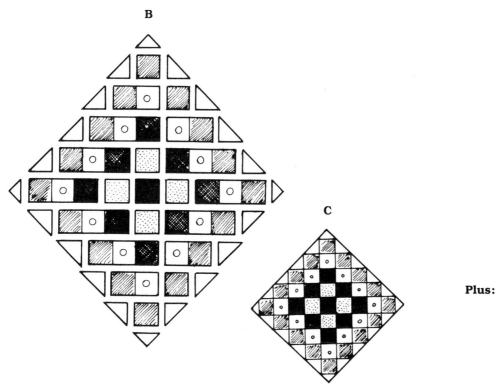

C

Figure 2

Assembling the Quilt Top

This is a diagonal set quilt. Please refer back to the Pink Mosaic Crib Quilt (page 59) for complete information regarding techniques used for diagonal set quilts, then proceed.

1. From the navy print fabric, cut:

- One piece 16 by 80 inches.
  From this piece, cut five 16-inch squares. Cut each square in quarters diagonally to obtain twenty setting triangles. (This includes two extra; the quilt requires only eighteen setting triangles.)
- Twenty 1¼-inch alternating plain squares.
- Two 8½-inch squares.

Cut each of these squares in half diagonally to yield four corner triangles.

2. Assemble the blocks into diagonal rows. Join the rows.
3. From the red print border fabric, cut four 5½ by 39-inch strips. Seam two strips end to end to make one border long enough for each end of the quilt top.
4. Matching the center seam of the border strip with the center point of the quilt side, stitch one border strip to the tip toward the border; trim the excess border fabric even with the sides of the quilt. Repeat to add the remaining border strip to the opposite edge of the quilt top.

Quilting and Finishing

Layer and quilt as desired. Cut approximately 325 inches of 3-inch-wide strips for binding. Refer to Chapter 11 for tips on applying French-fold binding.

Some Other Options

One of the advantages of strip techniques is the pattern-piece-free approach. You can decide to change the size of something simply by changing the size of the starting strip.

The Tennessee "Hard Times" or Cobblestones quilt block is fairly common. The little squares are sometimes as small as 1 inch or as large as 1¾ inches. Each row is finished with setting triangles so that the blocks can be set diagonally with alternating plain blocks. If you would like to use different size strips to make the same block, this chart tells you the approximate finished sizes.

Approximate measurements:

Width of cut strip or square*	1.5″	1.75″	2.0″	2.25″
Individual finished square	1.0″	1.25″	1.5″	1.75″
Finished design block	7.0″	8.75″	10.5″	12.25″
Diagonal of finished design block	9.8″	12.25″	15.0″	17 +″

*This is also the unit measurement.

Cobblestones Tote Pocket

If you want to add something special to a purchased canvas tote, make just one block; layer, quilt, border, and line it. Then top-stitch it in position for a wonderful pocket. If your sewing machine has a free-arm feature, that will make the sewing easier, but you can squeeze this through without.

Did you notice that in the quilt the block is on point, and now the block is setting flat but the interior squares are on point?

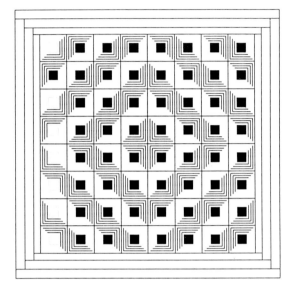

Figure 1

Red and White "Barn Raising" Log Cabin

Circa 1895–1900—probably from Texas

APPROXIMATE SIZE:
    86 × 86 inches

MATERIALS NEEDED:
    Scraps:
        2¾ yards light fabrics
        3½ yards dark fabrics
    1 yard red accent fabric
    ⅜ yard center square fabric
    ½ yard each of three border fabrics, cut crosswise

The Log Cabin block has been extremely popular since its inception in the mid-1800s. Folklore attributes the name to the building it portrays. Just as the settlers built their cabins with interlocking logs around a central chimney, quilters construct a Log Cabin block with fabric "logs" around a center square "hearth." The center square is often red to suggest warmth, and it usually remains the same size and color throughout the quilt. The Log Cabin block is

most often made diagonally divided into light and dark halves by using dark fabrics for the logs in half of the block and light fabrics for the opposite side.

The emphasis on dark and light makes the block especially conducive to the use of scraps. By simply varying the fabrics, "log" width, center square size, and the set of the blocks, you can make quilts with greatly differing looks. The strong diagonal design line in each Log Cabin block allows very interesting arrangements. The sets are so distinctive that many of them have their own names.

The red and white quilt shown here was constructed of sixty-four 9¼-inch-square log cabin blocks (Figure 1). As is traditional, the block is divided into light and dark halves. The center squares are the same size and color, and in this quilt they are twice as wide as the strips that form the "logs." However, the quilt departs sharply from tradition by including two red strips of gingham in an L on the otherwise light halves of the blocks.

The blocks are set eight by eight in the traditional Barn Raising pattern. The light and dark halves of the blocks form concentric light and dark diamonds, which are said to represent a barn's framing timbers laid out on the ground before the barn is erected. The red gingham L formations make a very interesting secondary pattern. The quilt is completed by an 8-inch border of three fabrics.

The materials list and instructions are for the size shown, which is square, as many antique quilts are. This size looks nice on a bed with pretty pillows at the headboard, or is very nicely used as a large wall quilt. If you prefer a longer quilt with a deep pillow tuck, add sixteen more blocks, a row of eight at both the top and bottom. The quilt will be approximately 88 by 106 inches. If that seems a little large, reduce the borders slightly.

Selecting the Fabrics

Approximately forty-five fabrics were used for the strips for the sixty-four blocks. The distinctive red gingham L on the light half of the block and the deep rust center square are used in all the blocks. Each block needs seven additional "log" fabrics—three light and four dark. This quilter chose complementary browns and a little navy, with gold, green, and rust accents for the dark halves. Fabrics with very light white or tan backgrounds were selected for the light halves. Select a center square fabric and accent fabric if you want to make a statement with a color. The quilt can also be made without that accent in the light side if desired. (See the Pinwheel Log Cabin on page 85.)

Cutting the Fabrics

Some people use templates and cut the center square and each strip for the Log Cabin block individually. You can do that, but strip piecing is faster, easier, and almost always more accurate. It is certainly my method of choice and the method I recommend for you. Cut your selected fabrics into 1½-inch-wide strips. Then cut the strips of center fabric into sixty-four 1½-inch squares. (Pattern pieces for templates for each strip and the center square are provided; see at right and on next page.)

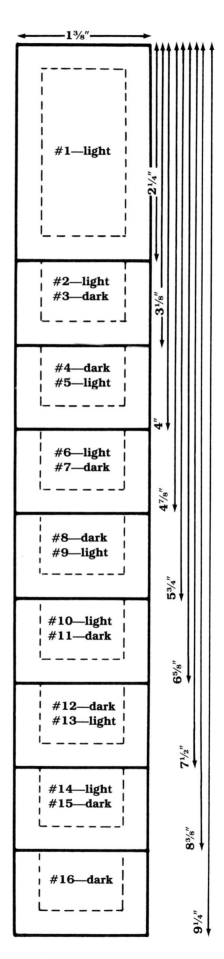

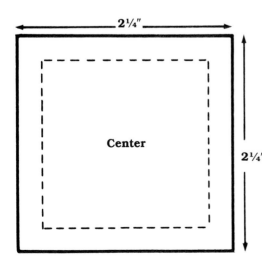

2¼″

Center

2¼″

Ensuring Accuracy

Cut your strips accurately and sew them together with a consistent ¼-inch seam allowance. Remember, however, that having ⅞-inch "logs" is more important than having perfect ¼-inch seam allowances.

Check your blocks as you go. A block may be undersize because the strip you have just attached is too narrow, either at one point or along its whole length. If the strip is no more than ¼ inch too thin, it is possible to compensate by making a very narrow seam when the adjacent strip is added. The adjacent strip will be slightly wider than normal; the two strips together will be accurate. Do not use a seam allowance less than ⅛ inch.

Obviously, if the last strip you attached is too wide and makes the block too large, you can simply trim the strip carefully to the correct width before attaching the adjacent strip. But be sure to double-check your measurements—comparing what you have with what you should have and what the rest of your blocks are—before being satisfied that the cure has worked and before adding any more strips.

Assembling the Block

As shown in Figure 2, the block is assembled spirally around the center square. In this quilt, each fabric was used twice, added consecutively to make a pair of "logs" that form an L shape. If you are using an accent fabric, it will always be used in positions 9 and 10. Select strips of the center square fabric, the accent fabric, three light fabrics, and four dark fabrics for your first block. Random use of scraps allows you to include as much or as little of a particular fabric as you want or have. Don't be surprised if random placement is a little hard to do at first. Because you have already divided your fabrics into light and dark shades of colors, this block is not as random as it sounds.

It is not necessary to backstitch at the end of each seam, as the next seam will cross over these stitches. After adding each piece, press its seam allowance away from the center square.

Refer to Figure 3 for the following steps.

1. Place the center square on top of the first strip of light fabric, right sides together and raw edges aligned. Seam and cut as shown. Press open and press the seam allowance away from the center square.
2. Rotate the two-piece unit as shown and sew again to the same light fabric, right sides together and one edge aligned. Cut and press.
3. Rotate the three-piece unit as shown and sew to the first strip of dark fabric, right sides together and one edge aligned. Cut and press.
4. Rotate the four-piece unit as shown and sew again to the same dark fabric, right sides together and one edge aligned. Cut and press.
5. The first round of strips is complete. Check the dimensions of the square. It should measure 4 inches by 4 inches. Check if you need to adjust the size by trimming the square, taking a smaller seam, or even changing a strip. Look for problems—and solve them—after completing each round of strips. Don't add strips to an inaccurate, out-of-shape block!
6. Continue to attach two strips of each fabric in the order shown in Figure 2 until all sixteen strips have been attached and the block measures 9¼ inches square. If you want to emulate the look of our quilt, remember to use the accent fabric in positions 9 and 10.

Assembling the Block with Chain-Piecing Techniques

You can work on several units at a time without stopping and breaking the thread to start again—just butt the next piece up to the previous piece. That is called chain piecing. (See Figure 4 for the Pink Mosaic Quilt, page 59.)

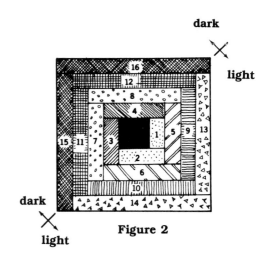

Figure 2

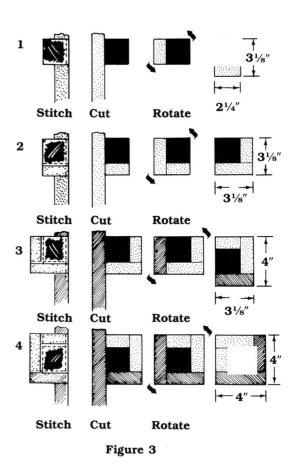

Figure 3

Some people think of chain piecing primarily as a technique to speed up the process of quiltmaking. It is that, but other important benefits are consistency and accuracy. From the second unit sewn, to the last one, there is always a unit for comparison. By matching the position of the parts and watching for visual discrepancies, your blocks should be more consistent.

Assembling the Quilt

1. Trim the blocks to a consistent size before joining them together. Each should be exactly 9¼ inches square, but it is quite likely they will vary in size, some smaller, some larger. Select a size to which all of your blocks can somehow be adjusted (trimmed down, a strip replaced, a smaller seam stitched), and then adjust the blocks that need it. Your goal is sixty-four blocks of the same size.

2. Lay out the blocks in the Barn Raising arrangement shown in Figure 1. For security, you may label the blocks with pieces of masking tape, identifying their positions before picking them up again. But first, look back at the pairs, pairs of pairs, and so on method of combining blocks described for the Red, White, and Blue String-Pieced Quilt on pages 26 and 28.

3. Now try this: Position the second row of squares face down on the first, and then pick those pairs up from the bottom of the quilt to the top, placing each subsequent pair of blocks on top of your stack. Take the stack to the machine and chain-piece. Make sure you are seaming the edge that was between rows 1 and 2. Do not cut the threads, but lay the blocks back down. They should be chained in position.

Proceed to put together the other rows and pairs of pairs, waiting until the end to make the one long seam.

4. Try to practice directional pressing. Alternating the direction of the seams in adjacent rows reduces bulk where the seams meet when the rows are joined.

Adding the Borders and Finishing the Quilt

The borders on this quilt, from the inside out, are 3 inches, 3 inches, and 2 inches. The last border is rolled to the back for the binding. Most likely this quiltmaker cut all borders the same width and then decided just to roll the last border to the back, making it smaller. (See Chapter 11 for finishing instructions.)

Antique "Barn Raising" Log Cabin with Hex Border

Circa 1885–1895

APPROXIMATE SIZE:
    66½ × 76½ inches

MATERIALS NEEDED:
    Scraps for the blocks:
        1¾ yards light fabrics
        1¾ yards dark fabrics
        ¾ yard red accent fabrics
    200 different 5-inch squares for the hexagon border
    Or **scraps totaling approximately 2½ yards**

This antique quilt (Figure 1) and the previous Log Cabin quilt are both set in a "Barn Raising" pattern and share the distinctive use of red "logs" in the light halves of blocks. There the similarities end. This is a much more structured Log Cabin unit, with a very unusual border!

While there are thirty-six Log Cabin blocks, there are ten different block combinations that repeat rigidly in this quilt. The positioning of the fabrics in these blocks is not random. To recreate this look, you must reuse a specific group of the fabrics in particular positions in different basic blocks. As an example, the bright red fabric appears in the centers and as an L in the light halves of some blocks, only as an L in other blocks, and not at all in the remaining blocks. Even the quilt itself is not assembled randomly; the position and orientation of the basic blocks in the quilt are fixed.

The quilt is finished with a unique hexagon border, 7 inches wide on two sides and 12 inches wide on the remaining two sides. Different scrap fabrics were used for practically every one of the nearly two hundred hexagons!

The size of this quilt makes it best suited for use as a wall quilt. You might want to make a smaller wall quilt by simplifying or eliminating the hexagon border.

Selecting the Fabrics

A limited number of fabrics were used and reused for the ten basic blocks. Follow the keying shown in Figure 2 to approximate the look of our quilt. Cut red centers for blocks A through D and light centers for the remaining six basic blocks. Make the light halves of blocks E through J identical, and use red fabric for strips 7 and 8 in the light halves of blocks A through D. Use random dark fabrics (in our case, browns and blues) in all the blocks. The blocks are labeled A through J. Make eight each of A and B, and four each of C and D. While the chart shows two each of E through J, they are so similar, that all twelve could be made alike.

Cutting the Fabrics

Using a rotary cutting system or scissors, a ruler, and a marker,

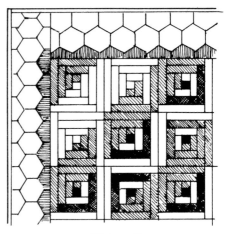

Figure 1

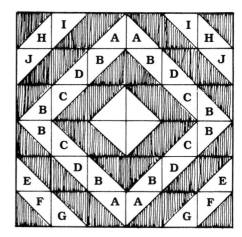

Figure 2

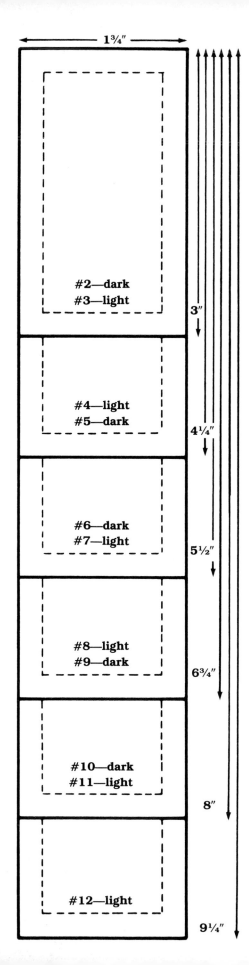

cut the "log" fabrics into 1¾-inch-wide strips. Cut the center fabrics into 1¾-inch squares.

Assembling the Block

Read the instructions on "Ensuring Accuracy" and "Assembling the Block" for the Red and White Log Cabin Quilt. Following steps 1 through 6 on page 77 and referring to Figure 3, assemble the blocks spirally around their center squares. Use a standard ¼-inch seam allowance and press the seam allowances away from the centers. Because you will be making more than one of each block, using the chain-piecing techniques and completing one color combination before starting the next would be an easy way to keep order.

Check the accuracy of your blocks as you go. Since the center square and the "logs" in this quilt are a different size than in the Red and White Quilt, the size of the blocks after each round of strips will be different. Also, this block only has three rounds. The blocks should measure 4¼ inches square after the first round, 6¾ inches square after the second round, and 9¼ inches square after all twelve strips have been added and the block is complete.

Assembling the Quilt

1. Trim the blocks to a consistent size before joining them together. Each should be 9¼ inches square. A different size is fine as long as all the blocks are that size; your quilt will simply be larger or smaller. Your goal is thirty-six blocks of the same size.

2. Lay out the blocks in the Barn Raising arrangement shown in Figure 2. Label the blocks with pieces of masking tape, identifying their positions, before picking them up again.

3. Assemble the horizontal rows, stitching the blocks together with ¼-inch seams. Press the seams to one side. Alternating the direction of the seams in adjacent horizontal rows reduces bulk where the seams meet when the rows are joined.

4. Join the six horizontal rows with ¼-inch seams.

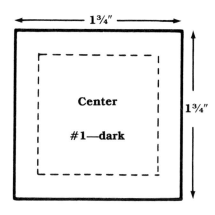

Adding the Borders

The hexagon border looks as if it might have been someone's intention to make a Charm Quilt, with every hexagon a different fabric. But the patchworker's impatience with the slow process and need for a border for this Log Cabin coincided and suddenly a potential quilt top became a border.

Using the hexagon pattern provided, make a full-size pattern by tracing the cutting size onto a stiff (preferably acrylic or plastic) material that can be cut with scissors or a knife. It is probably worth the effort to cut another piece the exact finished size so that you can mark both the cutting and sewing lines.

Cut between 180 and 200 assorted hexagons. Stack several pieces together and use the rotary cutter if your mat is permanent enough. Then go back and mark the sewing lines. Cut twenty-nine hexagons from a solid fabric. Cut the solid-color hexagons in half as shown on the pattern.

Decide whether borders will be two or three hexagons wide, and work accordingly. Lay out hexagons as desired, or work with a random placement.

HEX BORDER LOG CABIN PATTERNS

Cut here
for half blocks

1. Work the rows in the arc arrangement shown. Laying two hexagons right sides together, sew one ¼-inch seam, stopping ¼ inch from the edge of the fabric on each end of the seam (Figure 3).

2. Attach a third hexagon to the first two with another side seam, so that you have an arc of three hexagons connected by two seams. Press both seams in the same direction.

3. Continue making arcs of three hexagons until you have twenty-eight rows.

4. Take two rows of hexagons and fit the first seam together (Figure 4). Place these two rows right sides together; pin and sew the first seam, starting and stopping ¼ inch from the outside edges. You may find that you will need to remove your first or last stitch later, but that is easier than the alternative. Now remove the fabric from the machine and adjust the hexagons to sew the next seam. Continue, making five seams in total, always starting and stopping ¼ inch from the outside edges.

5. Stitch another row of hexagons to the first two rows and continue in that manner until the borders are as long as the center section (approximately fifteen rows).

6. Press both seam allowances in the same direction, not open, and press so that they spiral and make a pattern of three diamonds on the inside seam allowance (Figure 5).

7. The quilt pictured has two borders that are three hexagons wide, and two borders that are two hexagons wide. If you want equal-width borders, repeat as above, except the borders will be approximately twenty hexagons long. If you choose to make the two narrower borders, repeat steps 1 through 6, but make the strips only two hexagons wide and twenty long.

8. The contrasting frame around the Log Cabin center is made with matching solid-color half hexagons. Sew the half hexagons together end to end to the necessary length for each section.

9. Attach rows of half hexagons along the appropriate edge of hexagons in the same one-seam-at-a-time approach as step 4 above (Figure 6).

Adding Borders and Finishing the Quilt

The borders were added with blunt seams at the corners. See Chapter 11 for additional finishing information.

LOG CABIN PILLOW MEDLEY

The pillows on the next page are both considered Log Cabin variations. The techniques used are similar to those used for the quilt, in that you are sewing strips around a center square. All of the strips and center squares are cut 1¾ inches wide. No pattern pieces are needed when using strip techniques, so none are given.

Each pillow needs just a few scraps. Ours were leftovers collected from another project (see World Without End, page 117). Pillow-finishing techniques are given in Chapter 11.

Figure 3

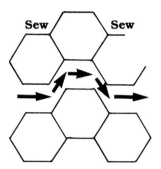

Figure 4

Figure 5

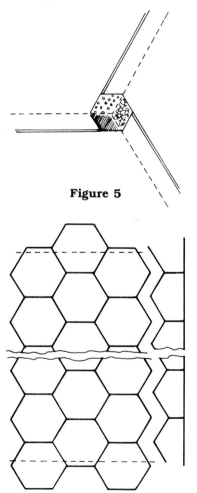

Figure 6

Log Cabin Pillow

APPROXIMATE SIZE:
  16¾ inches square
  Plus 1¾-inch ruffle all around

Make four blocks with three strips on each side of the 1¾-inch center square. Refer to instruction given for the Red and White "Barn Raising" Log Cabin, page 74. Join the four blocks with the dark sections to the center. Layer and quilt as desired.

Look at the picture and illustration again. Did you notice that the strips on the pillow rotate counterclockwise and the strips rotate clockwise in the blocks on both antique quilts? It doesn't matter, as long as you are consistent within each project. Also, starting with the light strips is my preference, because the block has a larger percentage of strips in darker colors that are more lively and interesting.

Log Cabin

Courthouse Steps Pillow

APPROXIMATE SIZE:
  16¾ inches square
  Plus 1¾-inch ruffle all around

The Courthouse Steps construction also works from the center block out, but instead of spiraling and having one half of the block light and one half dark, you add the matching strips to opposite sides of the center square, creating a double diagonal with four sections, two of which are light and two dark. The pillow is made with four Courthouse Steps blocks.

Courthouse Steps

Pinwheel Log Cabin

APPROXIMATE SIZE:
   82 × 102 inches

MATERIALS NEEDED:
   Scraps totaling approximately 7⅝ yards:
      3½ yards light fabrics
      4 yards dark fabrics
      ⅛ yard center square fabric
   ⅝ yard inner border fabric
   ½ yard each of three fabrics for middle border set
   1¾ yards outer border fabric
   ¾ yard binding fabric
   Forty-eight 11½-inch squares of backing fabric
   Forty-eight 11½-inch squares of bonded polyester medium weight
      batting plus batting for borders

The traditional, highly popular Log Cabin block that you learned to strip-piece in Chapter 7 can also be made with the Quilt-As-You-Sew method. The earth-tone quilt shown here was constructed of forty-eight different 11-inch-square Log Cabin blocks and a 10¾-inch border (Figure 1). Each block features the same deep rust center square and is divided diagonally into traditional light and dark halves. Because the center square is the same width as the strips that form the "logs," the dark and light halves of the block are divided by visually pleasing "perfect stair steps."

The blocks are set in a pinwheel pattern, six by eight. In this quilt, the backing square fabrics were chosen and the blocks arranged to form a checkerboard pattern on the back as well.

Selecting the Fabrics

Approximately thirty-six fabrics were used for the strips and backing squares for the forty-eight blocks. The colors were chosen from a limited palette: subdued brown, gold, green, rust, and turkey red "darks"; tan and ecru "lights." Choose five light and five dark fabrics for each block, in addition to a center square fabric.

Cutting the Fabrics

Using a rotary cutting system or scissors, a ruler, and a marker, cut your selected fabrics into 1½-inch-wide strips. Cut the strips of center fabric into forty-eight 1½-inch squares.

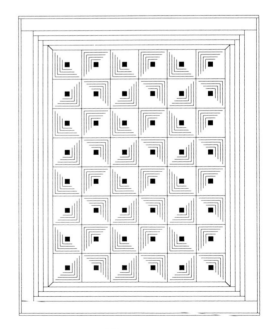

Figure 1

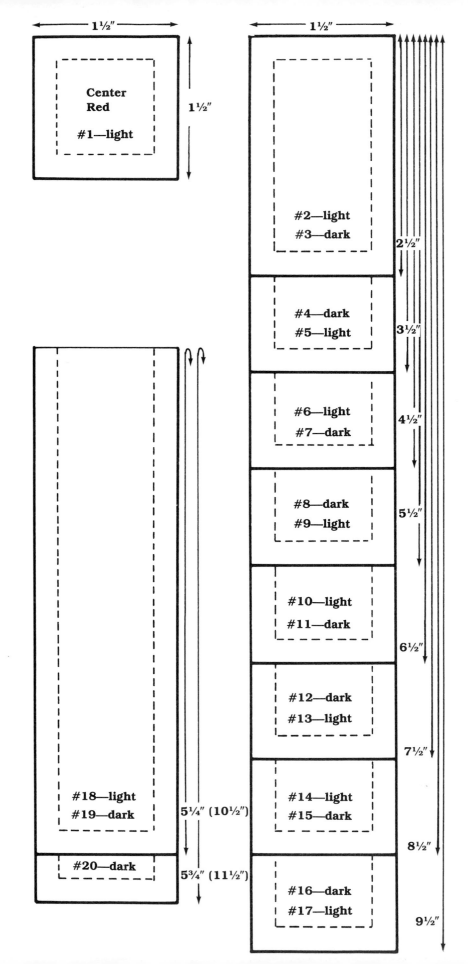

1½″

Center
Red

#1—light

1½″

1½″

#2—light
#3—dark

2½″

#4—dark
#5—light

3½″

#6—light
#7—dark

4½″

#8—dark
#9—light

5½″

#10—light
#11—dark

6½″

#12—dark
#13—light

7½″

#14—light
#15—dark

8½″

#16—dark
#17—light

9½″

#18—light
#19—dark

5¼″ (10½″)

#20—dark

5¾″ (11½″)

Cut forty-eight 11½-inch backing squares from these same fabrics. To duplicate the checkerboard pattern on the back of the text quilt, cut twenty-four from light fabrics and twenty-four from dark fabrics. Also cut forty-eight 11½-inch-square pieces of batting.

Assembling the Block

"Quilt-As-You-Sew" implies that you seam and quilt at the same time, stitching through top fabric, batting, and backing fabric as you sew each piece of your block together. That is correct. However, for the Log Cabin design (Figure 2), I recommend traditional machine piecing for the first five pieces, creating a 3½-inch center unit, and then proceeding Quilt-As-You-Sew. It is much easier to center accurately and sew the larger 3½-inch square on an 11½-inch square of batting and backing fabric than it would be with a tiny 1½-inch center square!

Select strips of the center square fabric, five light fabrics and five dark fabrics (Figure 2).

1. Read the instructions on "Ensuring Accuracy" and "Assembling the Block" given in Chapter 7 for the Red and White "Barn Raising" Log Cabin Quilt. Following steps 1 through 4 on page 77, construct the center unit for this block by piecing strips 1 through 4 to the center square.

2. Check the size of the center unit. It should measure 3½ inches by 3½ inches. Because everything builds around the center unit, it is crucial that it be truly square. Carefully press the square. Using a square acrylic template with printed grid lines and a rotary cutter, trim and straighten it. If you have only a ruler, pen, and scissors to do this task, consider cutting a cardboard template to check your square and use for marking the cutting line.

3. Place the batting on the backing fabric, right side down. Pin diagonally in the corners to stabilize them. Now center the previously pieced square on top and pin it in place. There should be 4 inches on each side (Figure 3).

4. Attach piece 5 with the Quilt-As-You-Sew method (Figure 4). Line up a strip of the second light fabric with the top of the center unit, right sides together and raw edges aligned. Stitch the seam through all four layers. After stitching, flip the strip away from the center unit so its right side is exposed. The seam that holds the layers together makes an indentation that holds the strip down; pressing with an iron may not be necessary. Instead, simply finger press at the corners. Now trim the strip to length. Leave a little extra fabric. Because you have to lift the strip away from the batting to cut it, you may not be as accurate as you might expect.

Notice that when you lay down a new strip, the edge that will not be sewn is a visible guide to be lined up parallel to a previously sewn strip. As shown in Figure 5, if the distance between the unsewn edge of the strip and a previously sewn seam is equal at both the top and the bottom, the new strip is parallel. (The unsewn edge of the new strip is useful in another way: When stitching the strip in place, use it as a guide for sewing straight.)

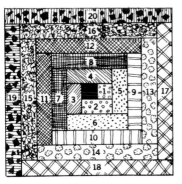

Figure 2

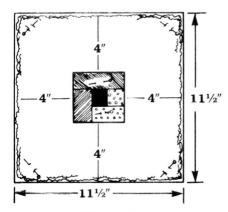

Figure 3

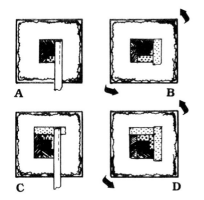

Figure 4

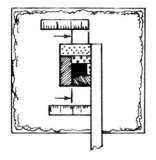

Figure 5

Figure 6

5. Turn the block 90 degrees counterclockwise and, in the same manner, stitch a strip of the same light fabric to the block to form piece 6. Repeat with the next dark strip for pieces 7 and 8 (Figure 4).
6. Having completed the first round of strips using the Quilt-As-You-Sew method, lightly press the block to make sure the four strips are flat for the next round of stitching. Turn the block over and clip the threads off the back so they don't get tangled in the next row of stitching. Now check the dimensions of the square. Do you need to adjust the size by taking a seam, or even changing a strip? Look for problems—and solve them—after completing each round of strips. Don't add strips to an inaccurate, out-of-shape block!
7. Proceed in the same manner to attach the next three rounds of strips. When done, the block should measure 11½ inches square.

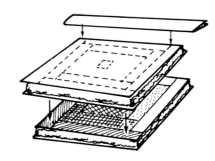

Figure 7

Assembling the Quilt

1. Trim the blocks to a consistent size. Each should be 11½ inches square. A different size is fine as long as all the blocks are that size. Your goal is forty-eight blocks of the same size.
2. Lay out the blocks as in Figure 6, so the dark halves of the blocks form pinwheels. If you used several contrasting fabrics for the backing squares, check the arrangement on the back of the quilt also (see the photo at right). When pleased with the arrangement, label the blocks with pieces of masking tape to identify their positions before picking them up again.
3. Assemble the blocks into horizontal rows, using finishing strips to sew the blocks together so no raw edges show on the back. For this quilt, cut forty strips 1½ inches wide by 13 inches long. Press the strips in half lengthwise, wrong sides together. Layer two adjacent blocks, right sides together. Now place a folded strip on the blocks, aligning all raw edges (Figure 7). Pin in place and stitch ¼ inch from the raw edges through all eight layers (see Figure 8, next page).

Pull the block firmly over your knee to open up the seam, and trim away the excess batting in the seam allowance between the layers of

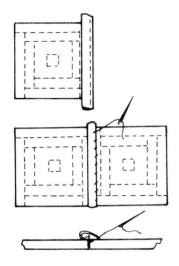

Figure 8

← **Finished strips**

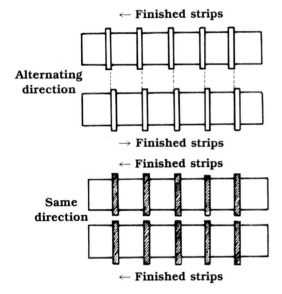

Alternating direction

→ **Finished strips**

← **Finished strips**

Same direction

← **Finished strips**

Figure 9

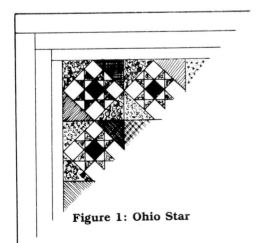

Figure 1: Ohio Star

fabric. You need not cut away fabric, except at the ends of the blocks where the next seam will be. Press the strip to the side so that it covers the raw edges and hand-stitch it in place with a hidden stitch.

The finishing strip is always pressed toward (and hand-stitched to) the block it did not touch when sewn (Figure 8). If the finishing strip contrasts with one or both of the backing squares, it is important to decide on which square you wish the strip to lie and to take care to pin it to the appropriate block before stitching.

Alternating strip direction in adjacent horizontal rows reduces bulk at the seam intersection when the rows are joined. Not alternating strips allows you to develop a grid system that lines up and creates a nice secondary pattern on the back of your quilt (Figure 9).

4. Join the eight horizontal rows with finishing strips. Cut seven strips of fabric 1½ inches wide by 75 inches long. (Piece as necessary to get the length.) Proceed as above, considering desired strip direction when selecting the fabrics for the finishing strips and before pinning a finishing strip to the rows of blocks to be joined.

Adding the Borders

For adding borders, see Chapter 11, page 139, "Adding Borders Quilt-As-You Sew." The finished border widths for this quilt are 2¼ inches, 1 inch, 1 inch, 1 inch, and 5½ inches. The three 1-inch borders were sewn together and added as a unit with a mitered corner. The other borders have blunt corners. As always, your choice of fabrics could change the arrangement, number, or proportions of attractive borders.

Ohio Star

APPROXIMATE SIZE:
  80 × 100 inches

MATERIALS NEEDED:
  ⅜ yard dark fabric (for center squares)
  ⅝ yard light fabric (to surround the center square)
  Thirty-five pieces at least 8 inches × 9 inches (light fabrics)
  Scraps, up to thirty-five medium and dark fabrics (equivalent to approximately 12 yards) for the front and back
  Thirty-five 12½-inch squares of batting
  ½ yard innermost border fabric
  ⅝ yard second border fabric
  ⅞ yard third border fabric
  1¼ yards outer border fabric

Fabric Selection

The two common fabrics in every block of our Ohio Star Quilt (Figure 1) are the center floral and the light background print surrounding the floral square. They were selected first. The criteria for selecting the rest of the fabrics was, "A fabric can be used if it isn't *ugly* with these two." It is very important to note that the remaining fabrics were not selected because they looked pretty with the constant two, they just couldn't look awful! Then it was just a matter of going through the fabrics in the studio and pulling enough light, medium, and dark fabrics. The star points were either medium or dark, the square surrounding the star was light. The large corner triangles were also medium or dark.

It wasn't necessary to have a very big piece of anything, although you will see that we used the same fabrics to make a scrap back, too.

Cutting by the Traditional Method

The number of pieces needed and the description of the scraps to be used are listed for each pattern piece (Figure 2). Use pattern pieces A, B, and C to cut the following:

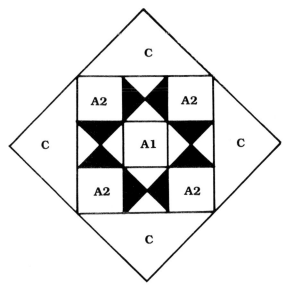

Figure 2

A1	(35)	matching centers from one fabric
A2	(140)	four each of thirty-five different light fabrics
B1	(140)	all matching from one light fabric
B2	(140)	four each from same fabrics as A2 above
B3	(280)	eight each from thirty-five different medium dark to dark fabrics for the star points
C	(140)	assorted dark fabrics (cut as many as thirty from medium darks for a little sparkle)

Using the Speed-Cutting Method

Using the rotary cutter system and multiple layers, cut as directed. You will be taking advantage of cutting triangles from squares. Some are cut two from a square, some are cut four from a square. That is because after analyzing the triangles, you can see that we want the straight grain on the hypotenuse of some and on the leg of other triangles. When you want the straight grain on the hypotenuse, speed-cut four triangles (double diagonals) from a square. When you want the straight grain on the legs of the triangle, speed-cut two triangles from a square (Figure 3).

The first cut on all of these pieces is squares, the number in parentheses is how many squares to cut.

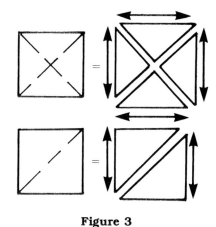

Figure 3

A1	3″ sq.	(35)	matching centers from one fabric
A2		(140)	four each of thirty-five different light fabrics
B1	3⅝″ sq.	(35)	from one light fabric to make 140 triangles
B2		(35)	from thirty-five different light fabrics to make 140 triangles—to match A2
B3		(70)	two each of thirty-five different medium dark to dark fabrics to make 280 triangles for star points
C	6¼″ sq.	(70)	assorted dark fabrics to make 140 triangles (Cut as many as fifteen from medium darks for a little sparkle.)

Piecing the Ohio Star Traditionally

If you want to make a scrap quilt but prefer to quilt using the traditional method, you may choose to assemble this quilt using the traditional nine-patch breakdown (Figure 4).

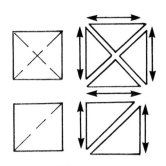

Figure 4

Prepiecing Ohio Star Subunits for Quilt-As-You-Sew

When you are making the Ohio Star using the Quilt-As-You-Sew method, you join the subunits in an entirely different way (Figure 5).

1. For the first subunit, begin with one 3-inch square (A1), and four triangles made from 3⅝-inch squares (B1). Piece together as shown in Figure 6. Place the right side of one triangle to the right side of the square, and sew in place. Sew another triangle on the opposite side of the square. Press both seams and triangles out. Position and sew the other two triangles in place. Press the seams and triangles out.

2. For the second and third subunits, use two 3-inch squares of the same fabric (A2), and four triangles of the same fabric cut from 3⅝-inch squares (B3). Place two triangles, right sides together, on adjacent sides of one square. Stitch, then press seams and triangles away from the square. Repeat for the third patch (Figure 7).

3. Subunits 4 and 5 use two 3-inch squares (A2), four triangles (B2), and four more triangles (B3). Attach one triangle (B2) to one triangle (B3) as illustrated in Figure 8. Do this four times. Press the seam toward B3. Now attach two triangles (B3) to adjacent sides of a square (A2), as shown in Figure 9. Make two complete sections for the fourth and fifth subunits.

4. The final corner pieces are four triangles cut from 6¼-inch squares (C). These triangles will be attached when you complete the Quilt-As-You-Sew.

Special tip: By adding four corners like this to any straight set block, you can turn the block into a quilt that looks like a diagonal set without needing to learn diagonal set techniques.

Quilt-As-You-Sew

1. Place a 12½-inch square of batting on a 12½-inch square of backing fabric that is right side down. Pin in place. Make sure this is perfectly centered before you go any further. Center the center subunit (from Figure 6) on top of the batting (Figure 10).

2. Place second and third subunit (from Figure 7) on opposite edges of your square, with right sides together and raw edges even. Stitch (¼-inch seam allowance) through all four layers—two patchwork sections, batting, and backing—as illustrated in Figure 11. (See the boxed note on page 89 if you encounter problems with the batting getting caught on the needle or presser foot.) Open out and finger-press at the corners.

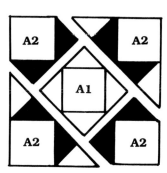

Figure 5

Figure 6

Figure 7

Figure 8

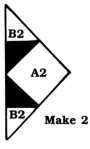

Make 2

Figure 9

Figure 10

Figure 11

Figure 12

Figure 13

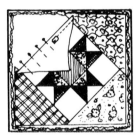

Figure 14

3. Place fourth and fifth subunits (Figure 9) right sides down on long edges of the previous work, as illustrated in Figure 12. With raw edges even, stitch through all layers and open out (Figure 13).

4. Place one of the large triangles (C) right side down and raw edges even, on the edge of the previous work (Figure 14). Stitch through all layers. Repeat on the other three corners.

5. Complete thirty-five blocks in this manner.

Assembling the Quilt

Follow the directions for assembling the Pinwheel Log Cabin Quilt-As-You-Sew, steps 3 and 4, page 87.

Borders and Binding

The borders we selected for our quilt became part of the controlling features of the quilt. The first border neutralized the large collection of prints and colors. The next three borders and the binding developed a color story that united the fabrics used. The borders were cut 2½, 3¼, 3¾, and 5 inches and were added Quilt-As-You-Sew. (See Chapter 11 for finishing details.)

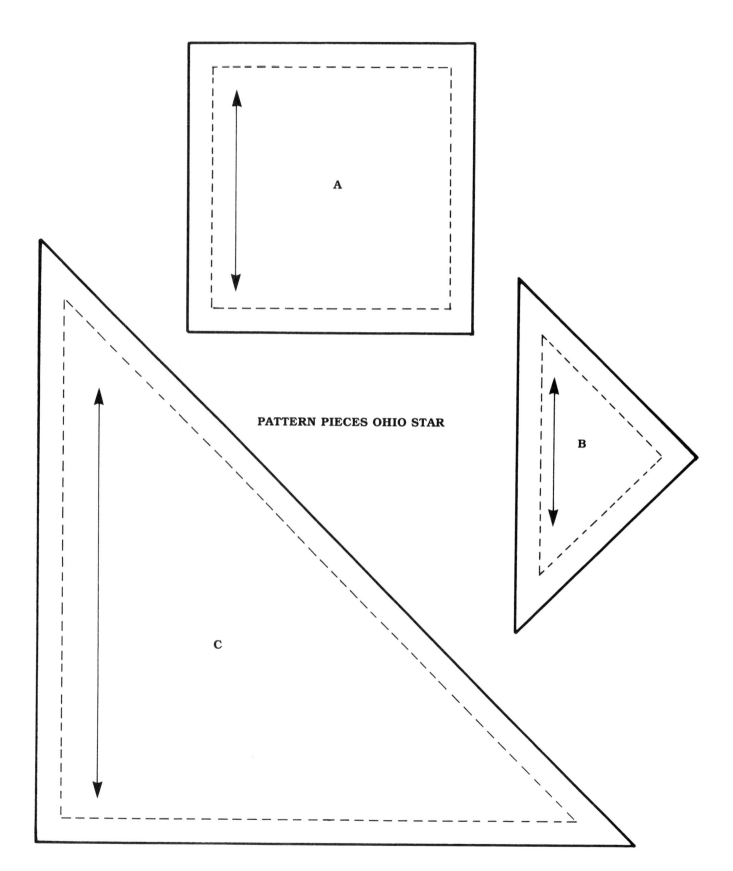

PATTERN PIECES OHIO STAR

95

CHAPTER 9

Appliqué Scrap Quilts

Appliqué is the process of stitching a decorative layer of fabric to a base layer. There are many different ways to appliqué. Both of the methods described here are by hand.

Freezer Paper Appliqué

This technique incorporates the use of freezer paper for ease and accuracy and is as quick as any hand appliqué. The freezer paper prevents the appliqué from distorting and seems to force your needle to take tiny stitches.

1. Cut freezer paper the exact finished size of the desired design.
2. Rough cut the fabric to approximately the size of the design with a ³⁄₁₆-inch seam allowance.
3. Center the freezer paper on the fabric with the unwaxed surface of the paper touching the wrong side of the fabric.
4. With the point of your iron, press the edge of the fabric over the edge of the paper. The fabric will stick lightly to the waxy surface, but it won't make your iron stick (Figures 1 and 2). Clip and notch seam allowances as necessary.
5. Position on the surface fabric and appliqué in place with a hidden stitch that *just* catches the edge of the appliqué (Figure 3).
6. Remove the paper piece as you approach the starting point, or stitch all the way around, then cut away the background fabric from behind the appliquéd design and slip the paper piece out.

Soft Hand Appliqué

Some people find they like a softer feel and want the fabric to be more pliable in their hands. This method satisfies those desires.

1. Mark the sewing line of the shape on both the background material and the right side of the design material. On the fabric to be appliquéd, make sure you mark *just* outside the shape so that it will get turned under when sewn. Cut out the pieces to be appliquéd with approximately a ³⁄₁₆-inch seam allowance.
2. Turn the seam allowance under at the starting point and secure the appliqué fabric in place. (Try this first without pressing.)
3. Work around the piece with a tiny hidden stitch. Turn the edge under about 1 inch ahead of your stitching as you go along. Use your needle as a tool to help turn and use your opposite hand to hold the fabric in place.
4. To turn under sharp points, as shown in Figure 4, (a) sew all the way to the end of the point, (b) clip off most of the point, then (c) fold under the other edge and continue sewing.

Waxy side up

Figure 1

Figure 2

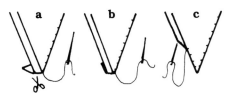

Figure 3

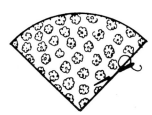

a   b   c

Figure 4

The Dresden Plate

APPROXIMATE SIZE:
    86 × 102 inches

MATERIAL REQUIREMENTS:
    400 petals are needed for the queen/double (twin, 300; king, 500)
        Individual petals require a piece 3 × 5½ inches
        If only using twenty fabrics, ¼ yard each is plenty
    4½ yards of background fabric cut into 16-inch squares (3⅝ for twin;
        5⅞ for king)
        Make twenty squares for queen/double, fifteen for twin, and
        twenty-five for king
    ¾ yard for first border (twin ½ yard, king 1 yard)*
    1 yard for second border (twin ¾ yard, king 1¼ yards)*
    1½ yards for third border (twin 1 yard, king 2 yards)*

    *All border measurements are for pieced borders.

During the great quilt revival of the 1920s and 1930s, the Dresden Plate Quilt was one of the favorite appliqué quilts. In general, scrap quilts are more likely to be patchwork than appliqué, but this appliqué quilt is particularly suited to scraps. In reality, the quilt shown has only twenty different prints in the petals, but random positioning gives the effect of more.

Figure 1

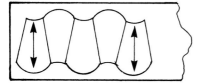

Figure 2

The instructions given are for a queen/double. The basic layout (Figure 1) adapts nicely to king and twin sizes. Just add five squares for the king and subtract five for the twin and make minor border adjustments. From here on, we will not refer back to changes for size, but will leave making those adjustments up to you.

Cutting

Cut at least twenty petals so that you can make the first Dresden Plate unit. Cut on the grain line as marked on the pattern. Take advantage of common edges when possible (Figure 2). Cut background squares or, if you prefer, one at a time as you complete each petal unit.

If you are using the freezer paper appliqué method, cut the necessary freezer paper petals, too.

Piecing the Dresden Plate

1. Select twenty Dresden Plate petals for the first square. Arrange the pieces in a pleasing order. Sew five pieces together. Press all seam allowances in the same direction, not open.

2. Use the layout on the next page to check accuracy. Your pieced quarter section should fit on this diagram. If it does not, the finished appliqué will not lie flat. Make any corrections necessary.

Make three more quarter sections, checking each one with the diagram. Then put the four sections together to make one complete Dresden Plate.

Appliquéing the Dresden Plate

1. The outside edges of the Dresden Plate must be turned under carefully and secured in place. Refer to the appliqué instructions at the opening of this chapter and decide which method you will use. Prepare the appliqué.

2. Find the center of the 16-inch square by folding it in half crosswise, then in half again. Where the folds cross, finger-pinch or mark the center with disappearing pen. Line up the quarters of the appliqué evenly with quarters of the square.

3. Use a hidden stitch to sew in place.

Assembling the Quilt and Adding the Borders

1. Assemble the blocks in four rows of five blocks each. Press the seams of your rows in alternating directions. Join the rows to complete the interior of the quilt.

2. There are three borders. From the inside out, the cut widths are 3¼ inches, 4 inches, and 5¼ inches. Measure your quilt carefully to determine the lengths to cut. Cut all the borders for the king ½ inch wider than the queen, and cut all the borders for the twin ¾ inch narrower.

Finishing

See Chapter 11 for additional information about borders and finishing.

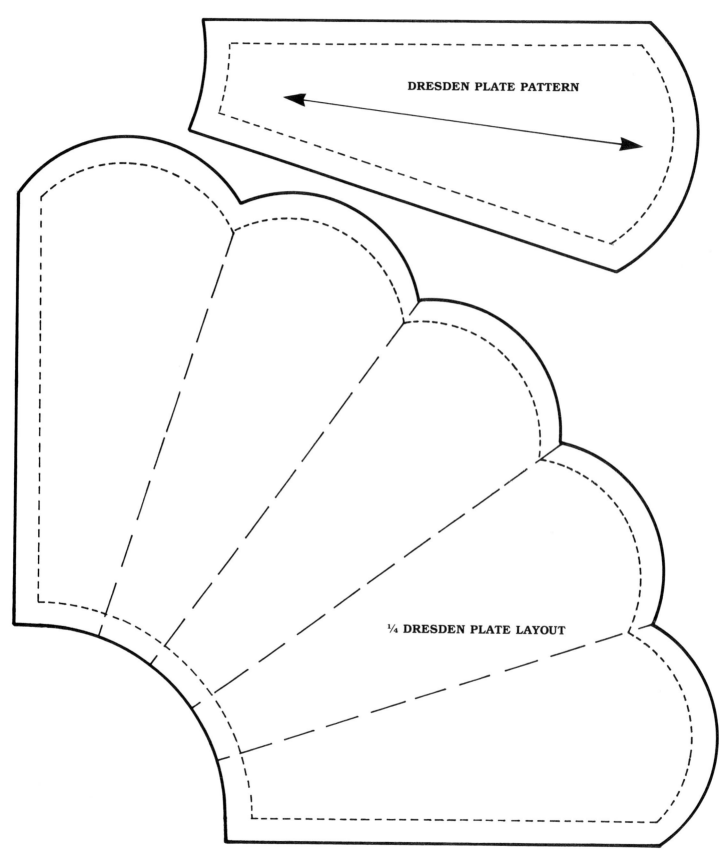

DRESDEN PLATE PATTERN

¼ DRESDEN PLATE LAYOUT

99

Helen's Purple Fans

APPROXIMATE SIZE:
    70 inches square

MATERIALS NEEDED:
    Four, twelve, and twenty of three different background squares $11\frac{1}{2}$
        × $11\frac{1}{2}$ inches
    Lots of purple scraps
    At least six different purple solids for the centers
    $\frac{3}{8}$ yard inner border fabric
    $\frac{1}{4}$ yard second border fabric
    $\frac{7}{8}$ yard third border and binding fabric
    Batting and backing, if working Quilt-As-You-Sew

When I was a senior in high school and a candidate for state 4-H officer, Helen Blaney was a young club leader in the neighboring township and accompanied us to the state convention. After college, I moved out of state. Helen raised a family and opened a fabric store, Back Door Fabrics, in Altoona, Iowa. As circumstances would have it, our paths did not cross again until a couple of years ago, when we had another opportunity to enjoy each other's company. Helen's store used to be an old hardware store, and it still includes lots of fixtures and some of the wares from its previous incarnation. When I stopped by, and as I was admiring the store, I noticed an unusual proportion of purple fabric. Helen told me that, as with lots of young girls, purple was her favorite color, and she just never outgrew it. Everyone teases her, but the customers know where to shop for purple.

It seemed the perfect opportunity for a surprise friendship quilt—get Helen's quilting students to do one block each, using at least one purple fabric bought at her store. Foiled by long distance, I finally decided the only way I could surprise her was to suggest the idea; she would have to organize it. I would come and teach an all-day class on scrap quilts, Quilt-As-You-Sew, invisible machine appliqué, and so on. Everyone was asked to bring purple scraps or scraps with purple in them to make a block for Helen's Purple Fan Quilt (Figure 1). So that's what we did.

Fabric Selection

Working with one color was a little different for me, as I usually work with a palette of colors. As I got ready to go to the class, I made a couple of false starts in trying to separate the warm purples from the cool purples, because they looked prettier together in individual fans. Intellectually I knew better—I'm writing the book, remember? This is a perfect example of the lesson that *really clashing is much better than almost matching*. Almost matching looks as if you don't know the fabrics don't really match, and the result is just irritating. Putting any fabric that included anything you could call purple into the potential pot really worked in this case.

It amazed the assembled group working on the quilt. They had

Figure 1

Figure 2

Figure 3

good-naturedly gone along with clashing and mixing the fabrics. After all, they were just making a block for someone else's quilt. It was a treat to see the surprise on their faces at the end of the day when we laid out thirty-six blocks; they loved what they saw!

Making the Fan

1. Using the fan pattern piece, cut seven segments for each fan. The pointed end is created by folding the broad end in half and, with the right sides touching and the end aligned, stitching ¼ inch from the end. Chain-stitch the seven you want for each fan to keep them together (Figure 2).

2. Clip a tiny wedge off the seam at the fold. Turn the point inside out so that the seam goes straight down the center of the section. Press. Stitch the sections together in the desired order. Press all seam allowances to one side.

3. Position the fan on the backing square and appliqué in place. The quilt photographed was actually made Quilt-As-You-Sew, so the fans were layered onto background fabric, batting, and backing squares. It was then appliquéd by stitching in the ditch with invisible thread between all of the fan segments.

4. Appliqué the heart center in place. With the quilt shown, we did an invisible machine appliqué, using a narrow machine hemming stitch and invisible thread. We stitched just off the edge of the piece to be appliquéd so that the hemming stitch would zigzag over and catch the appliqué (Figure 3). Add more quilting if desired. The pretty bow quilting design used on many of the blocks is included.

5. Arrange the fans as desired and assemble.

6. Add the borders. Cut widths of the borders are 1¾ inch for the inner gingham border, 1 inch for the muslin second border, and 2¾ inches for the third border. (See Chapter 11 for finishing information.)

7. The binding matches the last border and is ½ inch finished: That would be cut 2½ inches for the French fold method.

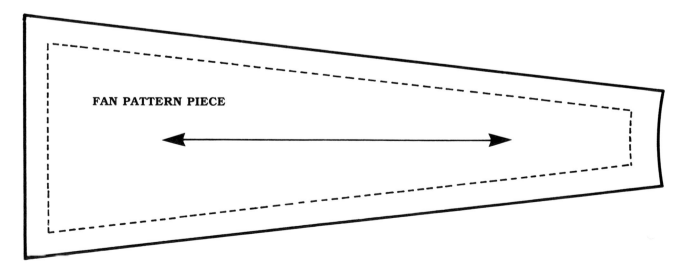

FAN PATTERN PIECE

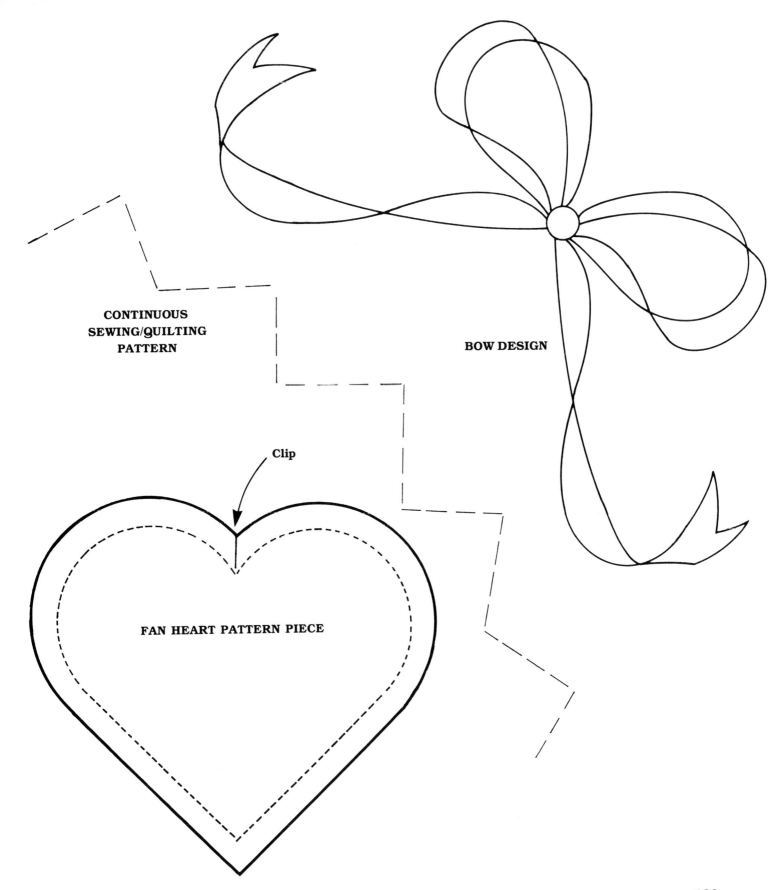

CONTINUOUS
SEWING/QUILTING
PATTERN

BOW DESIGN

Clip

FAN HEART PATTERN PIECE

Figure 1

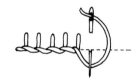

Blanket stitch
Figure 2

Outline stitch
Figure 3

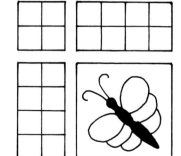

Figure 4

Mom's Butterfly Quilt

Circa 1935–1940, Iowa

APPROXIMATE SIZE:
    79 × 102 inches

MATERIALS NEEDED:
    2½ yards muslin background
    ¾ yard each pink and green for squares
    Seventy-five to a hundred scraps big enough for a butterfly and eight or twelve 2½-inch squares
    Block fabric
    Black embroidery floss

I can remember taking naps on this now worn-out Butterfly Quilt (in the background of our photo here). Actually, what I remember most is not the sleeping, but the game I always played trying to find matching squares of fabric before I went to sleep. Now that I think about it, I'm sure I was too old for naps, but Mom had found she could keep me quiet for a while on this fun quilt. I guess it was Mom who got me hooked on scrap quilts. Well, just one more thing I can thank her for.

This is Mom's Butterfly, not because she made it, but because she was lucky—she won it at a church raffle. It is typical of the late 1930s and early 1940s, appliquéd with the black buttonhole stitch around the edge.

Both the butterflies and the patchwork blocks in the sashing are random scraps. The controlling elements are the black thread, the muslin background, and the pink and green four-patch intersection units.

Making the Quilt

1. To position the butterfly, fold the background square diagonally and finger-press as a guide for the butterfly's line of flight. Embroider butterflies in place with a blanket stitch, using three strands of black embroidery floss. Using the freezer paper method of appliqué and the blanket stitch is a two-step process. Use freezer paper patterns, but appliqué all around the butterfly with what I call an appliqué basting stitch. That is a tiny hidden stitch, as for any appliqué, but in this case at least a half-inch apart. Remove the paper and then go around with the blanket stitch (Figure 2). Add the details with an outline stitch (Figure 3).

2. Piece the four-patch pink and green units. (See four-patch instructions given for the Pink Mosaic Crib Quilt, page 59.) The four-patch technique would also be an easy way to piece the scrap sashing strips. Just remember to keep them random.

3. Assemble forty-eight units as shown in Figure 4, and two extra lengthwise rows of sashing blocks, one for the bottom and one for the right side of the quilt. (Those for the top and left side are pieced with the units.) Combine units to complete the quilt top as shown. One extra row of sashing blocks (for the quilt bottom) should be thirty-six squares long by two squares wide, and the other row (for the right side) should be forty-eight squares long by two squares wide. The long row should begin and end with four-patch pink and green units, while the other only begins with the pink and green.

Finishing

Layer, quilt, and bind as desired (see Chapter 11).

Options

If you like the Butterflies but would prefer a few less, twenty-four blocks arranged four by six would be almost enough to cover the top of a double bed, and the quilt could be finished with borders. Nine blocks with sashing all around would make a nice wall hanging.

The Butterfly Pillow

Make just one appliqué and border with scrap fabrics for a pillow that will look great snuggled into a collection of pillows. This pillow is finished with a purchased 2¼-inch ruffle on top of a 3-inch ruffle that matches the butterfly.

BUTTERFLY PATTERN

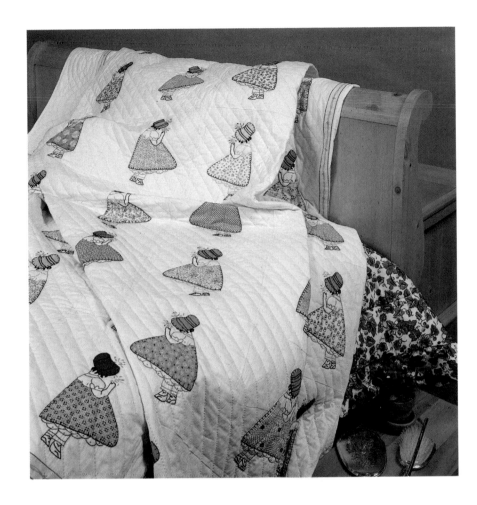

Little English Lady

Circa 1930–1935

APPROXIMATE SIZE:
   81 × 98 inches

MATERIALS NEEDED:
   7 yards muslin background for blocks, border, and binding
   Forty-two 6-inch scrap squares for dresses
   Forty-two 3-inch scrap squares for hats
   ½ yard for contrasting border
   Coordinating and black embroidery floss

If you really love embroidery and have a granddaughter, this quilt is for you (Figure 1). Composed of forty-two different print scraps for the dresses, coordinated with seventeen solid scraps for the bonnets, the controlling elements are the black thread, embroidered flowers, and the muslin background. (In the antique quilt shown in our photograph, some of the muslin blocks have discolored.) You will want the same fabric for all of the background and borders.

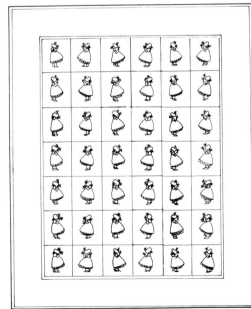

Figure 1

Outline stitch

Figure 2

Satin stitch

Figure 3

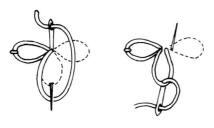

Lazy Daisy stitch

Figure 4

Making the Quilt

1. Cut forty-two blocks from muslin, 11 inches by 12¼ inches. Finished size will be 10½ inches by 11¾ inches.

2. Center and trace the pattern for the girl onto the muslin blocks, using either a light pencil mark or a "disappearing" pen. All of the embroidery will be done using two strands of floss. Using an outline stitch in a color coordinated with what you will be using for the dress and bonnet, embroider the blouse, petticoat, and pantaloons (Figure 2). Use a black outline stitch to embroider the shoes and arm. The hair is embroidered in black, using a tight satin stitch (Figure 3). A lazy daisy stitch in your choice of colors is used for the flowers (Figure 4). Details for the flowers and pantaloons are color-coordinated French knots (Figure 5).

3. Embroider the dresses and bonnets in place on the blocks, using black embroidery floss and following step 1 for Mom's Butterfly Quilt (page 104). Use a black outline stitch for the bonnet detail.

4. Assemble forty-two blocks into six vertical rows of seven, having three rows of seven girls facing to the left, and three rows of seven facing to the right (Figure 1).

Adding the Borders

There are two borders. The inside border has a cut width of 1⅝ inches; the outside border has a cut width of 7¾ inches. Measure your quilt top carefully to determine the correct lengths to cut.

Finishing

Layer, quilt, and bind as desired. (See Chapter 11 for details. A quilting pattern similar to the one used on the quilt pictured here has been included.)

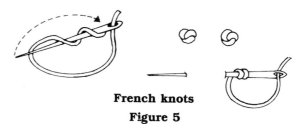

French knots

Figure 5

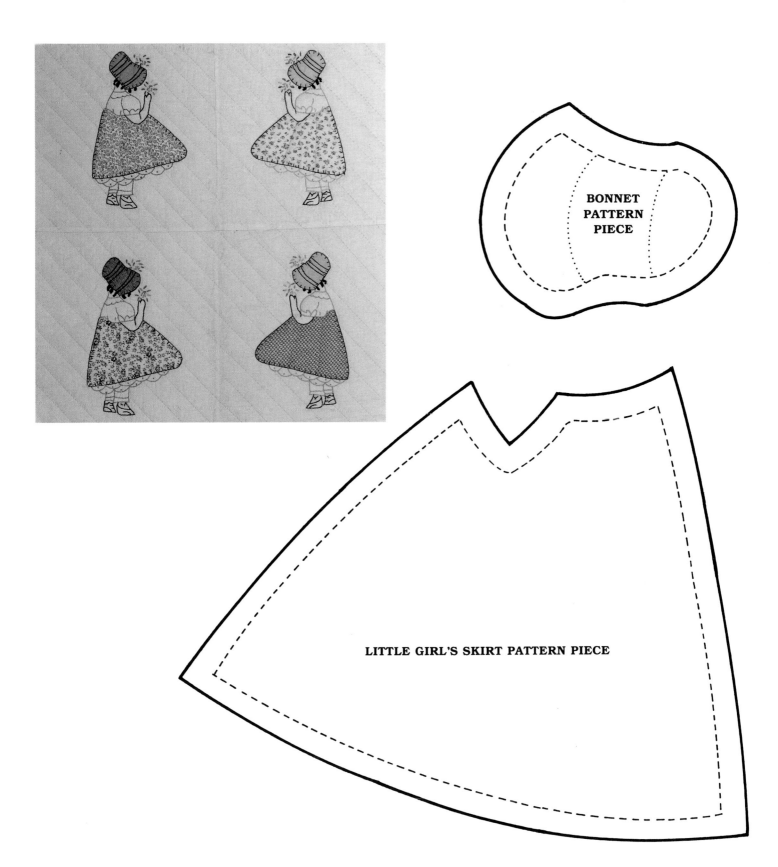

BONNET PATTERN PIECE

LITTLE GIRL'S SKIRT PATTERN PIECE

109

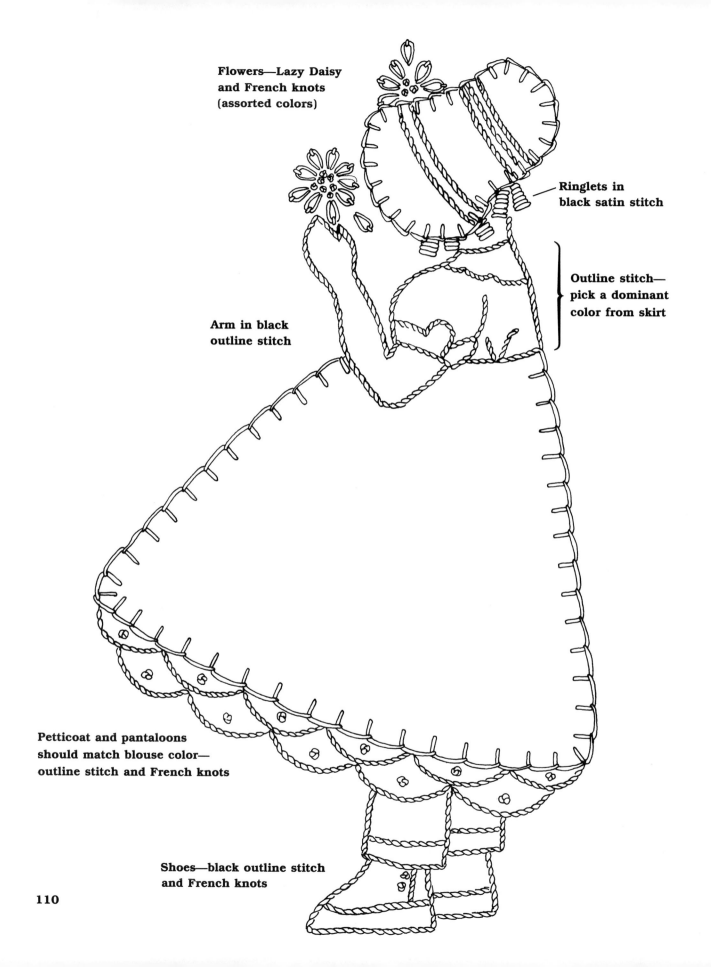

Flowers—Lazy Daisy
and French knots
(assorted colors)

Ringlets in
black satin stitch

Outline stitch—
pick a dominant
color from skirt

Arm in black
outline stitch

Petticoat and pantaloons
should match blouse color—
outline stitch and French knots

Shoes—black outline stitch
and French knots

110

CHAPTER 10

Other Piecing Techniques

Pinwheel Baby Quilt

APPROXIMATE SIZE:
   23½ inches square

MATERIALS NEEDED:
Quilt and pillow:
   1¼ yards of muslin or parchment fabric (includes quilt backing)
   Scraps of from six to nine different pink print and solid fabrics
   ¼ yard of pink polished cotton for inner border, binding, and pillow
      piping*
   ¼ yard of a dark print for the middle border*

   *This fabric can/should be repeated as one of the scrap fabrics.

Pillow:
   1 yard of narrow piping cord
   20 inches of ⅛-inch-wide satin ribbon
   Polyester filling

Making the Quilt

   Just because you're using small fabric scraps doesn't mean you can't take advantage of quick piecing techniques. The method for perfect-pieced right-angle triangles described here is both faster and more accurate than cutting lots of little triangles individually and sewing them together one by one. This little baby or doll quilt (Figure 1) is the perfect project for sampling the quick piecing technique. When following this method, you will mark and sew the triangles together *before* you cut them out.

   If this method is new to you, once you try it you'll never make triangle sets any other way. If you've done perfect piecing before, check these directions. Our method is slightly different from others; it eliminates directional problems with fabric design.

Making the Perfect-Pieced Triangle Grid

1. Count how many pieced squares you need. The number of squares you draw in the grid will be half that many, because you get two triangle pairs from every grid square.

   Measure the size of the pieced square (two triangles). To make the Pinwheel Baby Quilt and Basket Pillow, you need fifty-eight squares with a finished size of 1½ inches. Each Pinwheel contains four squares and finishes to a 3-inch square.

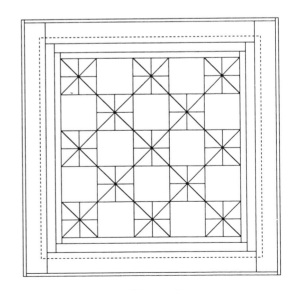

Figure 1

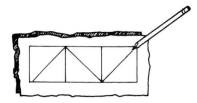

Figure 2

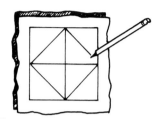

Figure 3

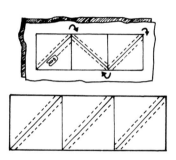

Figure 4

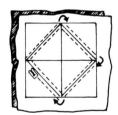

Figure 5

2. To properly allow for all seams, you will mark squares in the grid that are ⅞ inch larger than the measurement of the finished square. In this case, you want a finished 1½-inch square, so your grid will be made with 2⅜-inch squares. Don't throw up your hands about measuring such an odd amount. Today's wide acrylic rulers (which you use with the rotary cutting system) make measuring accurate and easy. Because you're working with small scrap pieces and want variety, you may mark only three or four squares on each grid (Figures 2 and 3).

3. Cut pieces of muslin the same size as your print scraps. Layer the muslin and scrap fabrics right sides together, with the lighter fabric on top. Leaving a small margin on all sides, use your ruler and marker to make horizontal lines 2⅜ inches apart. Use the same ruler to mark all the squares in the grid.

For this quilt, mark a grid on muslin of at least two squares to go with the darkest (middle border) fabric. Mark twenty-seven grid squares for the remaining scrap fabrics. When pieced, this will make fifty-eight squares.

4. Draw a diagonal line through each marked grid square, changing the direction of the line in each adjacent square (Figures 2 and 3). This enables you to stitch the grid continuously (without lifting the presser foot) and also eliminates potential problems with directional designs in fabrics.

Stitching the Perfect-Pieced Triangles

1. Stitch through both layers of fabric on both sides of the diagonal lines. Your seam allowance must be an accurate ¼ inch for the resulting squares to be accurate. Use the edge of your presser foot as a guide if it measures ¼ inch (Figures 4 and 5).

2. By marking this way, you can stitch an entire grid by only making 90-degree turns at the end of each row. When you complete one side of the lines, make a 180-degree turn and return on the other side. For the most efficient stitching in any grid arrangement, start at a corner that has a single diagonal line coming directly into it.

3. There are two pieced units in every grid square. Cut the triangles apart on every drawn line (Figures 6 and 7). Press the seam allowance toward the darker fabric. Sort the pieced squares into pairs of the same fabric combination.

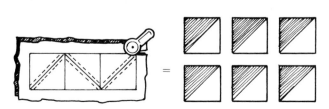

Figure 6

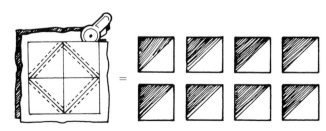

Figure 7

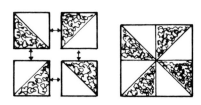

Figure 8

Making the Pinwheel Blocks

1. Select two pairs of squares for each Pinwheel and assemble as shown (Figure 8). Press the seam allowances toward the pink triangles. If all your seam allowances are pressed toward the pink fabric, the seam allowances in the middle of each pair will be going in opposite directions and will act as "automatic pins" in matching the seam lines.

2. Complete thirteen Pinwheel blocks. Make sure they spin in the same direction. Save one pair of pieced squares of the darkest scrap fabric for the Basket Pillow, plus three other pairs.

Joining the Pinwheel Blocks to the Alternate Squares

When you have thirteen Pinwheel blocks, you are ready to join them to the alternate fabric squares. It may seem as if the step of cutting these squares is omitted, but with the chain-piecing methods described in the instructions for the Pink Mosaic Crib Quilt (page 59), you will streamline the process of joining patchwork blocks to alternate squares. Instead of cutting the alternate squares first and then sewing them to the blocks one by one, you will sew the blocks to a long strip of the background fabric and then cut them. You gain perfect-size squares because you use the block as the cutting line for the alternate square.

Check the size of your blocks. They should be 3½ inches. If so, proceed. If the blocks are slightly larger or smaller but consistent, the quilt will finish larger or smaller, and you will need to make only minor adjustments as you proceed. If your squares are a different size, use that measurement instead of 3½ inches in the steps that follow.

1. To begin the chain-piecing process, cut one 3½ by 44-inch strip of muslin background fabric. Place a Pinwheel block on this strip, keeping right sides together and stitch, using the ¼-inch seam allowance, along the length of the muslin strip.

2. Place a second Pinwheel block on the fabric directly against the bottom edge of the first block, and stitch in the same manner. Continue placing Pinwheel blocks on the muslin strip and stitch them one after another. Sew twelve of the Pinwheel blocks in this way; the one block left over will go in one corner of the baby quilt.

3. When you have finished piecing, press the seams toward the muslin strip.

4. Now, using a rotary cutter, ruler, and protective mat, cut through the solid fabric strip. First "square up" your blocks. Put a horizontal ruler line on the seam line, center the block, and trim one side, if necessary. Repeat on the next side and with each block, cutting through the muslin as you work. You should now have twelve block/square combinations. The Pinwheels and the background squares are already joined and their edges should be even. You achieve much greater accuracy following this method than by cutting the alternate squares separately and then stitching them onto the blocks.

Keeping Things Simple

Many scrap quilts are made with just different arrangements of squares made of two right-angle triangles, one light and one dark. This makes hand-piecing triangles of a given size and putting them together to make a quilt very simple. For those of you who are a little more impatient, this is a wonderful way to machine-piece fabric scraps quickly and accurately.

I always say it isn't fair to learn how to machine-piece if you haven't first made something by hand, where you cut the triangles out, put them right sides together, and feed them through a sewing machine the old way, with their little corners catching on the feed dogs and distorting, and you pulling your hair out!

But then, life isn't always fair.

Assembling the Quilt Top

An efficient way to join the new subunits of one Pinwheel block and one alternate square is shown in Figure 9. Create three horizontal rows; then it's a simple matter to join the rows.

Adding the Borders and Finishing

1. Cut four 1¼ by 17½-inch strips of the solid pink fabric for the first border. Cut four 1½ by 19-inch strips of the dark print fabric for the second border. From the muslin, cut two 3½ by 19-inch strips and two 3½ by 24-inch strips.

2. Completing one fabric before starting another, add all borders in the same order, first to the top and bottom, then to the sides.

3. Layer the backing, batting, and quilt top; baste the three layers together. Quilt as desired by hand or by machine. When quilting is finished, add a separate binding of solid fabric (see Chapter 11).

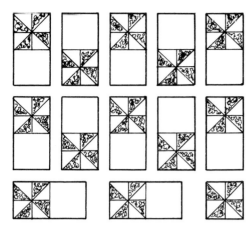

Figure 9

Basket Pillow

APPROXIMATE SIZE:
  7½ inches square plus 1-inch ruffle

We used fabric left over from the Pinwheel Baby Quilt to make a sweet little pillow, shown in the photo with the Pinwheel Baby Quilt. The only extras you'll need are cording for the piping, ribbon, and a small amount of washable polyfill.

Piecing the Basket Block

1. You should have eight perfect-pieced triangles left over from the baby quilt, including two with the darkest print fabric. From the remaining scraps of the darkest print fabric, cut one right-angle triangle with 3⅜-inch legs (seam allowance is included).

2. From the muslin, cut two 2 by 3½-inch strips, a 2-inch square, and four strips 1½ by 8 inches. Also cut one 2⅜-inch square, then cut this square in half diagonally to obtain two right-angle triangles. If your perfect-pieced triangles are slightly larger or smaller than our 2-inch measure, adjust the sizes of your pieces accordingly. Set aside a ¾ by 44-inch strip of muslin for the pillow ruffle.

3. Assemble as shown in Figure 9 for the Pinwheel Baby Quilt.

4. Add the 1½-inch-wide muslin border strips at the top and bottom edges of the block. Trim excess border fabric even with the sides of the block. Sew the remaining border strips to the block sides.

Adding the Piping

1. Use purchased piping if available, or cut a 1½-inch-wide by 36-inches-long bias strip from the solid fabric. (Piece shorter strips if necessary. An 8-inch square should make plenty of bias. See Chapter 11 for information on piecing bias.)

2. Fold the bias strip in half, wrong sides together. Put the cording in the fold, and, using a zipper foot, machine-stitch close to the cording.

Basket Pillow

3. Matching raw edges, baste the piping onto the Basket block: Lay the cording just outside the ½-inch seam line at the edge of the block. Overlap the ends of the piping where they meet, leaving the excess in the seam allowance.

Adding the Ruffle

1. Seam the ends of the ruffle strip together, creating a circle. Press this seam allowance open.

2. Fold the ruffle strip in half, wrong sides together. At the raw edge, stitch a row of machine basting ¼ inch from the edge. Make a second row of basting ½ inch from the edge. Pulling gently on the dangling threads, gather the ruffle strip to approximately 31 inches long.

3. Pin the ruffle around the outside edge of the pillow top, matching raw edges. Allow plenty of fullness at the corners. Baste the ruffle in place.

Finishing the Pillow

The pillow back should be the same size as the pillow top, approximately 8½ inches square. Use a scrap of muslin or any pink fabric for the back. Lay the back over the top, with right sides together. The basted ruffle and piping will lie between the top and backing. Sew around all sides, leaving a 3 to 4-inch opening in one side to turn the pillow right side out.

Today's good quality polyester stuffing has eliminated the need to make removable pillow covers, since the better brands of stuffing are washable. Just be sure you're using a washable stuffing. A layer of batting under the top (even if it's not quilted) helps to hide stuffing lumps.

Use a dull-pointed object (pencil, crochet hook, or the like) to poke out the corners and to push stuffing in. Stuff the pillow firmly, making it fuller than really seems necessary, as the stuffing tends to settle and flatten with time.

Close the opening with a tiny, invisible hand stitch.

World Without End

APPROXIMATE SIZE:
   78 × 96 inches

MATERIALS NEEDED:
   Scraps, equivalent to approximately 6 yards of fabric
   ⅞ yard of a light fabric for border 1
   ⅔ yard of a medium or dark fabric for border 2
   2 yards of a light fabric for border 3 and the binding
   8 yards for backing
   Polyester batting

Selecting Scrap Fabrics

More than a hundred different fabrics were used in making our World Without End Quilt. Each main block has a different combination of fabrics. While I had intended not to use any fabric in more than one block, I did end up using some of the light colors more than once. If there were no repetitions anywhere, the forty-eight basic blocks would use 144 different fabrics. Each basic block requires a combination of one light and two contrasting medium to dark fabrics. In addition, I wanted the fabrics that were going to be in the large triangles to be what generally are considered larger prints, and the medium or dark pieces to be a nice accent fabric against that print. The light fabric would always be in the background.

Selecting was rather time-consuming, but fun. However, when I got to the point of unfolding the fabric and cutting a very small amount just to put the rest back away, I began to have second thoughts. Those thoughts resulted in the "Five from One" project. (It actually started out to be "Three from One" and just grew.)

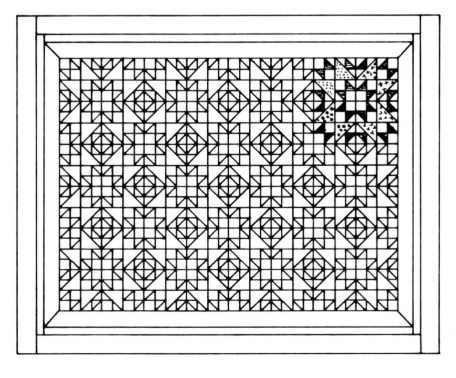

Figure 1

Five from One

Pulling over a hundred fabrics off my shelves just to cut a 6-inch square from each seemed like a lot of work. I decided to design some other quilts to make from the same fabric group, but it was important it not appear I had done that.

It was easy to keep the same three fabrics in a unit for the Blue Mosaic Quilt. They just got combined differently. Cutting the larger dominant print of each combination into an equal-size square helped to disguise that we were even using big prints. In the World Without End Quilt, the patchwork blocks are set together, touching, with no contrasting fabric to divide them. Having an important color as an alternating block gave a whole different look to the fabrics.

For the third quilt, I decided to cut two Log Cabin strips 1¾ inches wide by about 27 inches long from each medium or dark fabric, and four strips the same size from each light fabric. That would be enough to make the Pinwheel Log Cabin Quilt. As that quilt was already pieced, I put aside the strips for the real number 3 for a rainy day when all I want to do is sew, no cutting. The Log Cabin Medley of pillows was made from the strips.

Quilt 4 was the Bonus Crib Quilt. It came from the scraps of the Blue Mosaic and had teal added to give a different look.

Number 5 is Illusions, a quilt I had been wanting to make, but hadn't taken time to select fabrics for. Once I decided on the taupe and dark teal, I just cut 8 or 10 inches off the appropriate Log Cabin strips above. When you reduce those big prints down to 1¼-inch finished squares, it is really hard to recognize that the fabrics are the same.

Back to Victorian Shadows

Remember the Victorian Shadows Quilt shown on page 35? Now you can recognize that the method for piecing the squares was a version of this perfect-pieced triangle method. If you try to remember and transfer new techniques you learn in one project to later projects, your creativity and increased capabilities will make your quiltmaking even more enjoyable.

Cutting the Fabric

After you have selected the three fabrics to be included in each basic block, cut the following shapes. Cut the light fabric into one 3 by 12-inch strip (for pattern B), two 3⅜-inch squares, and one 3⅜ by 10⅛-inch strip (for pattern A). Cut two large triangles (pattern C) from the dominant contrasting fabrics. From the other contrasting fabric cut one 3⅜-inch by 10⅛-inch strip (also for pattern A). Once these have been cut, you are ready to put together the two small squares that make up the larger basic square.

Cutting Directions for "Three-in-One" Quilts

LIGHT BACKGROUND FABRIC

Quilt 1. World Without End*
  Cut one strip 3⅜ by 10⅛ inches to get six perfect-pieced triangles.
  Cut two 3⅜-inch squares to get four triangles the same size.
  Cut one strip 3 inches by 12 inches.
*You can cut all the pieces here from a piece of fabric approximately 10 inches by 12 inches.

Quilt 2. Blue Mosaic
  Cut two strips, 11 inches long by 2½ inches wide

Quilt 3. Log Cabin
  Cut four strips, 27 inches long by 1¾ inches wide

LARGER DOMINANT PRINT

Quilt 1. World Without End
  Cut one 6-inch square, then cut again on the diagonal to get two large triangles.

Quilt 2. Blue Mosaic
  Cut one strip 11 inches long by 2½ inches wide.

Quilt 3. Log Cabin
  Cut two strips 27 inches long by 1¾ inches wide.

ACCENT FABRIC

Quilt 1. World Without End
  Cut one strip 3⅜ inches by 10⅛ inches to get six perfect-pieced triangles.

Quilt 2. Blue Mosaic
  Cut one strip 11 inches long by 2½ inches wide.

Quilt 3. Log Cabin
  Cut two strips 27 inches long by 1¾ inches wide.

Figure 2

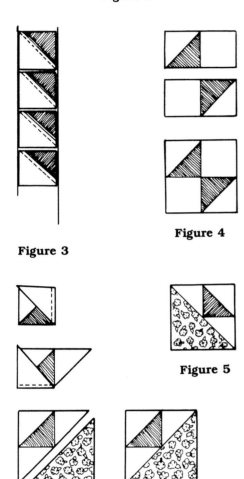

Figure 3

Figure 4

Figure 5

Figure 6

Figure 7

The Basic Block

Each basic block is formed by joining two each of two different subunits into a foursome.

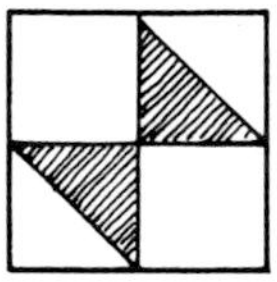

Making the First Subunit (Figure 2)

1. Using the perfect-pieced triangle techniques (pages 111 to 112), place the strip of the contrast fabric face down on the same size strip (3⅜ by 10⅛ inches) of the light fabric. Mark this strip to sew the perfect-pieced triangle grid. (If you are using a directional fabric, you will need to mark to account for directionality in the quilt blocks. See Pinwheel Baby Quilt, Figure 4, page 112.) Sew and cut apart on the drawn lines. You should have six squares. Press the seams to one side. Set aside two of these squares to be used in constructing the second subunit.

2. Take four squares and place them next to each other along the other strip (3 by 12 inches); cut from the light fabric, keeping right sides together (Figure 3). You must make sure you have all your squares facing the same direction along the strip as shown. Sew along the edge of the contrast fabric and the top edge of the strip. Carefully cut each square apart. Press the seams to one side.

3. Now take two of the rectangles you have just completed and place them, right sides together, with the squares at opposite ends as shown in Figure 4. Make a ¼-inch seam down one long side. Repeat with the other two rectangles and press seams to one side. This completes the first subunit.

Making the Second Small Subunit (Figure 5)

1. Take one of the remaining two squares you constructed from the light and the contrasting fabric. Place one small triangle of the light fabric on top of the square so right sides are together. Position the small triangle on top so that you can see both of the fabrics showing in the other half of the square below (Figure 6). Make a ¼-inch seam along the edge of the square where the two different fabrics are placed together. Press the seams to one side and open, with the small triangle pointing to the top.

2. Lay another small triangle of the light fabric on top of the square, right sides together, again positioning it so that you can see both of the fabrics showing in the other half of the square. Make a ¼-inch seam along the side of the square as shown in Figure 6. Press the seam to one side and open. You should now have one large triangle, with the contrasting fabric positioned in the "middle."

3. Now you are ready to join this patched triangle to the large triangles you cut using pattern C. Position the two triangles in place, with right sides together, and make a ¼-inch seam along the long edge of the triangle. Repeat to make two of these squares.

Making the Basic Block

Take the four squares you have just completed and arrange them as shown in Figure 7. Seam together in the arrangement shown and press seams to one side. This completes the basic block.

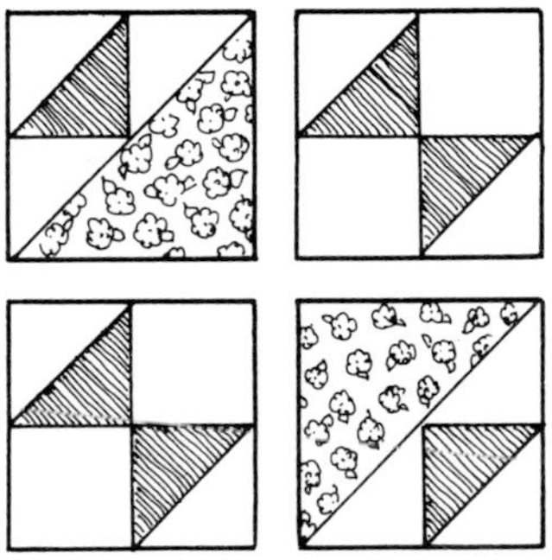

Joining the Basic Blocks

While the quilt looks very random, if you look more closely, you can see that in most foursomes the accent fabrics in the small triangles are from the same color family. Lay the blocks out and assemble the four blocks into a unit (Figure 8). Press the seams.

This large unit is now ready for quilting, if you want to make the quilt the way we did. Layer each large unit with backing and quilt "in the ditch" (see page 139). This can be done in one continuous line if you follow the stitching arrows in Figure 9. Then quilt the central star and the four corners in the arcs shown in Figure 10. Again, follow the arrows for continuous stitching ease.

Finishing

The block units are put together in four horizontal rows of three blocks each (Figure 11). Use finishing strips to assemble the blocks. (See directions for Pinwheel Log Cabin, page 85.) The World Without End Quilt borders were added using the Quilt-As-You-Sew method. The borders are 3, 2, and 5 inches finished width from the inside out, plus a ½-inch finished separate binding (see Chapter 11).

Figure 8

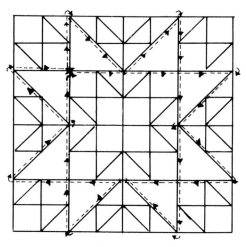

Figure 9

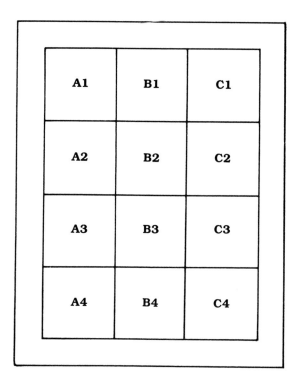

Figure 11

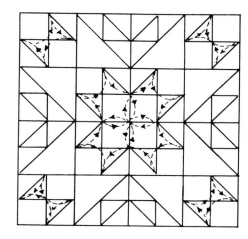

Figure 10

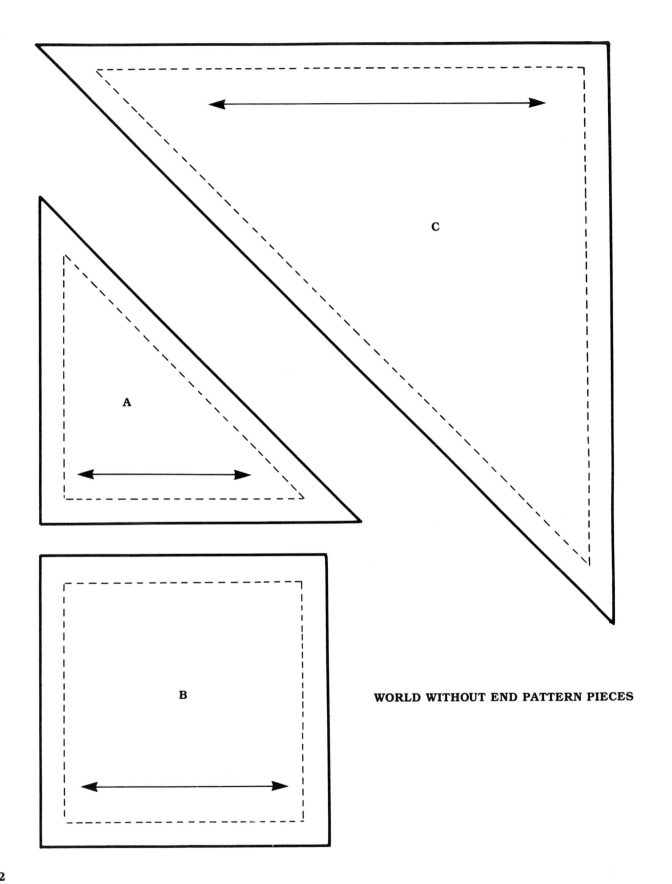

WORLD WITHOUT END PATTERN PIECES

122

Contemporary Star Quilt

APPROXIMATE SIZE:
   36 inches × 43 inches

I referred to this quilt by Ellen Rosintoski in Chapter 2 (page 12). If you compare the empty diagram (Figure 1) to the photograph, you will see that this quilt is certainly a study in the use of light and dark fabrics. The dark half of the quilt uses fabrics that create the "spinning footballs," while the light half of the quilt accents the "stars." To have done this with only eight fabrics is almost incredible. The repeated element of this quilt pattern is almost three vertical strips of nine blocks. Looking carefully, you will see that the quilt pattern is unbalanced: The last vertical strip of blocks in the third repeat is incomplete. It is the imbalance in the color story and the quilt pattern that gives this quilt such energy and feeling of movement.

Of course, no one could ever copy this quilt exactly. An important part of the delight of any quilt like this is that it is an original. To make your own original, inspired by Ellen's design, you will want to cut more shapes of each color than you actually will use. You will need the extra pieces because you will want to lay out the entire quilt before sewing anything, arranging and rearranging the colors until you are satisfied with the effect.

Once you have decided the layout of colors, piece each single block (this quilt contains seventy-eight pieced blocks and thirty solid blocks), and lay out the quilt again. You may be surprised to see how much a seam in a block can change the color arrangement from your original intention. When you are finally pleased with the look, piece the blocks into twelve vertical strips, and then piece the strips together.

This quilt was finished with a 4½-inch border and a ½-inch binding (see Chapter 11 for finishing details).

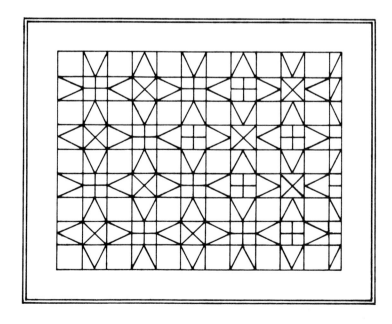

Figure 1

CONTEMPORARY STAR PATTERN PIECES

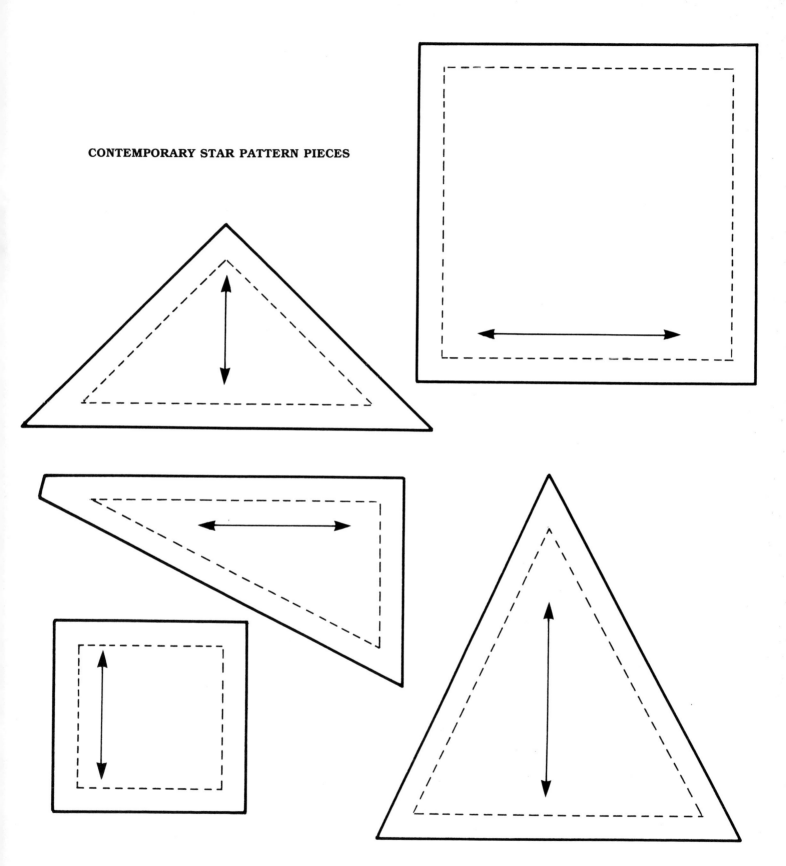

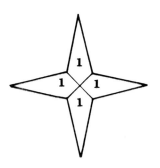

Figure 1

Figure 2

Mariner's Compass Quilt

APPROXIMATE SIZE:
    106 inches square

MATERIALS REQUIRED:
    Scraps to equal 6 to 8 yards of fabric
    9¼ yards background fabric for blocks and pieced borders
    1⅛ yards contrast fabric for appliqué
    ⅞ yard for unpieced 2-inch border
    ¾ yard for French fold binding

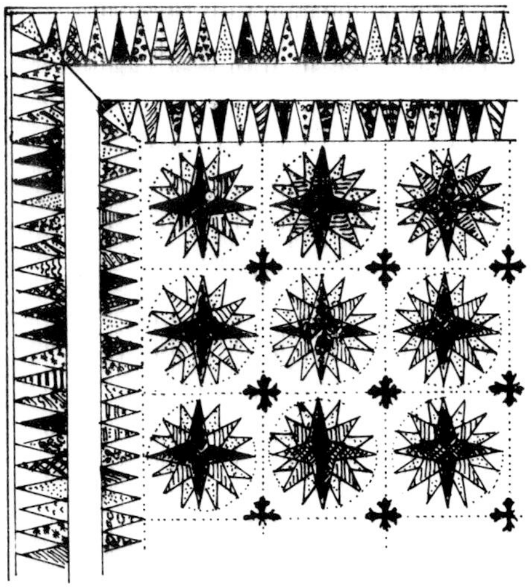

Bettina Havig is a founding member of the Booneslick Trail Quilters Guild in Missouri. For the past five years, members have drawn one name each month to choose a quilt pattern and colors, for which each member then makes one block. Bettina's choice was the Mariner's Compass Quilt (Figure 1), and she and thirty-five other members each completed one of the thirty-six blocks. Bettina provided the background fabric, and completed the border and appliqués spaced between the blocks. There are approximately 144 different fabrics used to make the compass blocks alone.

Fabric Selection

Bettina provided the background fabric and the following instructions for fabric selection: "Think of your fabrics on a scale of 1 to 10. If 10 is very dark and 1 is white/light, then don't use any color lighter than 5 on the scale. Don't use pastels; maintain subtle contrasts."

Cutting

The best way to complete a quilt of this detail is to use Bettina's method: Combine forces with thirty-five of your friends!

Otherwise, using the numbered pattern pieces provided, cut as follows:

1. Cut 144 from very dark assorted colors, four from each fabric.
2. Cut 144 from medium dark assorted colors, four from each fabric.
3. Cut 288 from medium dark assorted colors, eight from each fabric.
4. Cut 576 from background fabric.
5. Cut 144 from background fabric.
6. Cut 25 appliqué motifs.

Piecing the Quilt Blocks

Use the same fabric for each like pattern piece in each quilt block.

1. Join the four pieces of pattern 1, following the diagram shown (Figure 2). Be especially careful not to sew into your seam allowances when piecing the blocks. In fact, unless you're an expert machine-piecer, you'll probably have fewer headaches if you hand-piece this quilt. Set this "star" aside. Complete thirty-six "stars."

2. Join two of piece 4 to one of piece 3 to complete one of section A (Figure 3). Make eight of section A. Join two of these to adjacent sides of piece 2 to make one of section B (Figure 4). Complete four of section B.

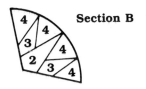

Figure 3 (Section A)

Figure 4 (Section B)

Figure 5

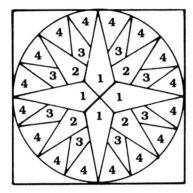

Figure 6

3. Join the four pieces of section B to the "star" from step 1 (Figure 5). For best results, begin your seam at the vertex of the angle.

4. Now add the four of pattern piece 5 to the compass to make one quilt block (Figure 6). Keep the four points of the star on the vertical and horizontal.

5. Complete thirty-six blocks in this manner.

Optional Method

You may choose to appliqué the completed compass circle onto a solid block rather than using the pieced method described in step 4. If you decide to do this, again, make sure you keep the star points of the compass on the vertical and horizontal.

Assembling the Quilt Top

You will probably want to lay out the quilt blocks and arrange the colors to your satisfaction.

1. Piece four blocks together in a two-by-two section. Appliqué the motif (pattern piece 6) into the center of this section, referring to the directions on page 96 for appliqué. Complete nine four-block sections.

2. Piece three of these sections together, and appliqué between them. Complete three of these twelve-block sections.

3. Piece these sections together and appliqué. You will have completed the quilt top, and will have appliquéd the motif between every quilt block.

Adding the Borders

The border for this quilt was also hand-pieced. A 2-inch-wide strip was used between the first and second pieced borders. In Bettina's quilt this 2-inch strip has mitered corners because the fabric used was a stripe.

1. Using the pattern piece given, for the first (inside) pieced border, cut a total of 168 light pieces (42 per side) and 172 dark pieces (43 per side). For the third (outside) pieced border, cut a total of 196 light pieces (49 per side) and 192 dark pieces (48 per side). Bettina used background fabric for the light pieces.

2. Sew the border pieces together as follows. The inside borders begin and end with dark pieces, alternating lights and darks. The outside border begins and ends with light pieces, alternating darks and lights. (All four sides of the quilt have equal-length borders.)

3. The corners of the borders are cut and pieced using the corner pattern pieces given. For the inside border cut the following to make four corner units (pattern pieces are given on page 132):

Piece A	cut four	from dark
Piece B	cut four	from light (background fabric)
Piece C	cut eight	from dark
Piece D	cut four	from light (background fabric)
Piece DR*	cut four	from light (background fabric)

*Piece DR is pattern piece D reversed (turned over).

For the outside border corner units cut the same number of pieces from each pattern but reverse the colors (dark becomes light and light becomes dark).

4. To piece the corner unit for the border, begin with piece A and attach to the short side of piece B (Figure 7).

5. Now take two of piece C and attach to pieces A and B as shown (Figure 8).

6. Pieces D and DR should be sewn together as in Figure 9.

7. Next piece the unit made from D and DR to the first unit made using pieces A, B, and C as shown (Figure 10).

8. Complete four border units using the color pattern for inside border and four border units using the color pattern for outside border.

9. Piece completed inside borders to edges of quilt and inset corner units by hand. Add the 2-inch border on all sides next. Next add the pieced outside border in the same manner as you did the inside pieced border, then add corner units.

Finishing the Quilt

This quilt was bound with a ½-inch French fold binding. Cut strips 2⅝ inches wide and apply.

Figure 7

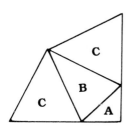

Figure 8

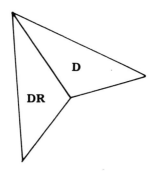

Figure 9

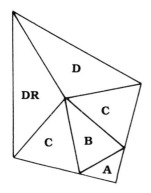

Figure 10

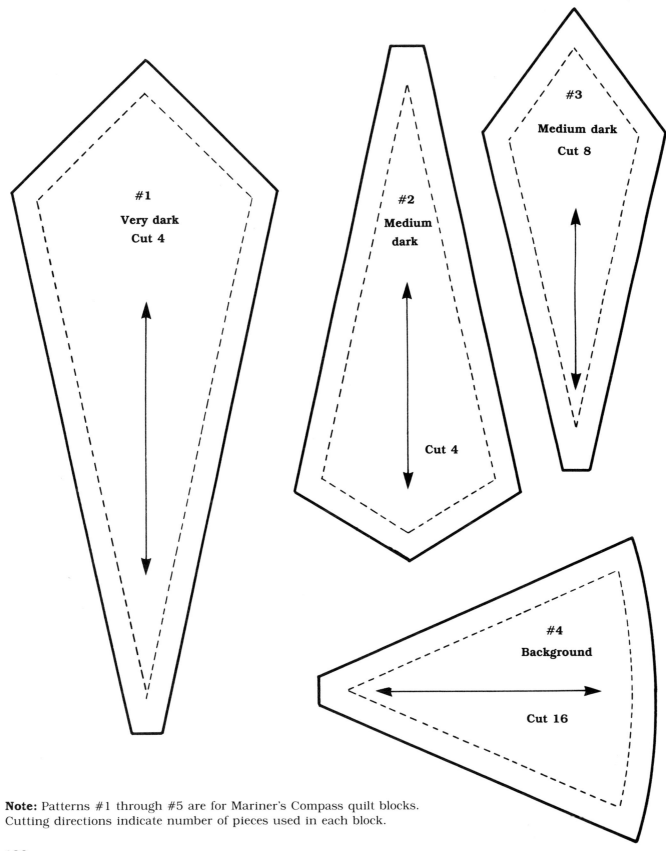

#1
Very dark
Cut 4

#2
Medium dark

Cut 4

#3
Medium dark
Cut 8

#4
Background

Cut 16

Note: Patterns #1 through #5 are for Mariner's Compass quilt blocks. Cutting directions indicate number of pieces used in each block.

130

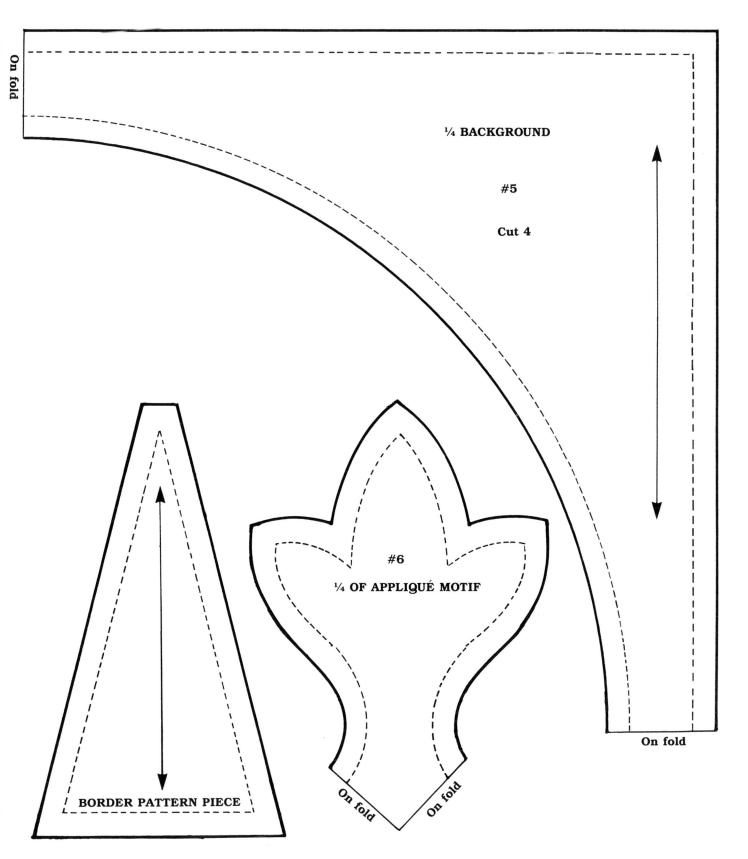

On fold

¼ BACKGROUND

#5

Cut 4

On fold

BORDER PATTERN PIECE

#6
¼ OF APPLIQUÉ MOTIF

On fold

On fold

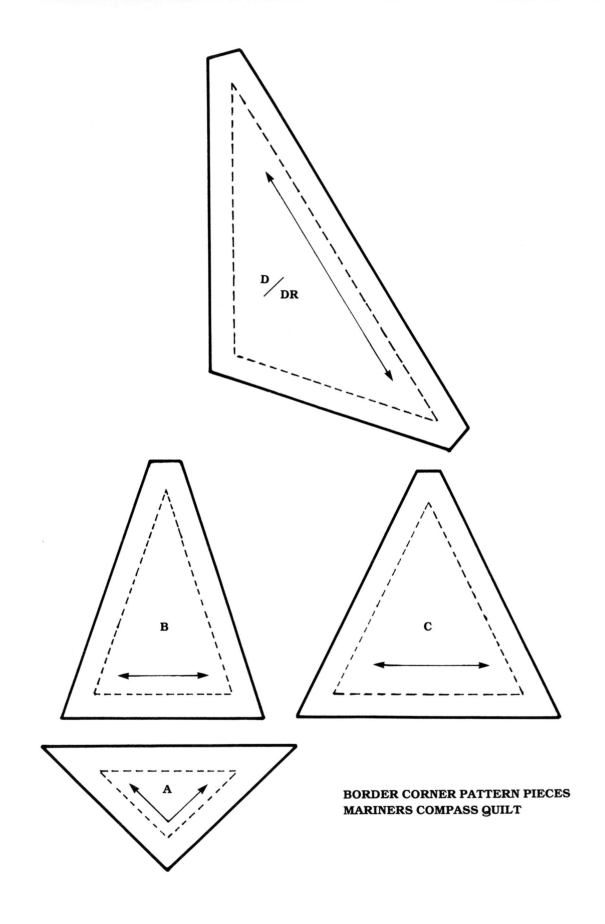

BORDER CORNER PATTERN PIECES
MARINERS COMPASS QUILT

CHAPTER 11

Finishing the Quilt

This chapter covers methods of finishing your quilt; establishes what size a quilt should be; specifies how to select borders, bindings, backings, and the like. I've included a special section for adding borders via Quilt-As-You-Sew—a wonderful method I use often but have never seen described in any book. You may want to spend a little extra time reading through that section.

WHAT SIZE SHOULD A QUILT BE?

If you are making one of the projects in this book, you will note the approximate finished size is included for everything shown. I encourage people to take a relaxed attitude about size and make quilts the size that looks best for them. Quilts don't have to go on beds. They don't have to go on beds in the same boring way when they do go on beds. However, since I don't expect to convince everyone of this, I am including sizes that I use when I want to make a quilt with a standard bed size in mind.

Except for the crib size, these guidelines were established adding a 9-inch pillow tuck to the length and a 13-inch drop to the other three sides of the most common standard mattress sizes.

Crib—*Small*, 30 inches by 45 inches; *Large*, 40 inches by 60 inches

Twin—65 inches by 97 inches

Double—80 inches by 97 inches

Queen—86 inches by 102 inches; *Queen/Double*, 84 inches by 100 inches

King—104 inches by 102 inches

When calculating, remember that compromises often have to be made. A 14-inch block doesn't always fit the perfect number of times in both directions, so as to leave the perfect amount on all sides for borders. Also allow 2 to 4 inches in both directions for the quilt to "shrink" when quilted.

BORDERS

Selecting Border Fabrics

The most important thing to remember about borders is that the sizes of the borders in this book are only a record of the borders on these quilts. They can be used as a starting point for the number and width of your borders, but they aren't the only right dimensions. In other words, because you will be using different fabrics, different balances may be needed to make the borders look right with the quilt and with each other.

While I usually have an idea what I will be using for borders, I never make a final decision until the quilt interior is done. It may have ended up a different size than expected, which would affect the width of the borders. With scrap quilts, it is common to have the quilt take on a different predominant color than you had planned. You may decide you want to emphasize that, or you may want the border fabric to override that color. You may be having so much fun making squares that you decide to go without a border (as with the Red, White, and Blue String Quilt).

Because I usually select borders from fabric I have in the studio, I lay the quilt out and try different widths of different combinations until I'm satisfied. If you have to go to the store to buy borders, take the quilt with you. Find a place where you can look at several different combinations without interfering with other customers, and do the best you can positioning bolts of fabric in sequence.

Try to Cut Borders on the Lengthwise Grain

Whenever possible, I cut borders in one piece on the lengthwise grain. However, it often is not practical to have that much fabric. For example, a 3-inch-wide border cut on the lengthwise grain would require 2 to 3 yards of fabric, but on the crosswise grain and pieced could be cut from ⅞ yard of fabric. In most cases, there would be only one seam.

Since you have to buy ⅞ of a yard of fabric anyway, why not buy a yard and a quarter (that's 45 inches long, the same as the fabric width) and cut the strips on the lengthwise grain. There will still be only one piecing seam, and you'll just have a little fabric left to make other scrap quilts.

Mitered Corners

There's a good chance you've noticed the omission of almost all mitered corners in my quilts. (Actually, because you are only seeing photographs, you may not have noticed.) When the same nondirectional fabric is being used in the entire border, the resulting corners look the same whether they are blunt-seamed or mitered (Figure 1). Blunt seams require much less fabric and time to make, plus I have a theory (which is, by the way, adaptable to other pesky things in life).

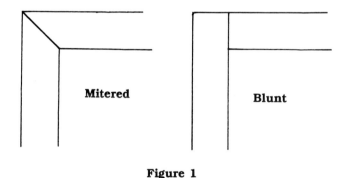

Mitered   Blunt

Figure 1

The Mitered Corner Quota Theory

I believe that we are all born with a quota for the number of perfect mitered corners we can make in a lifetime. I would hate to be eighty-five and have some great floral striped border fabric just begging to be mitered and have used up my quota mitering something as undemanding as muslin. So I save my mitering for corners where it really counts.

There is a corollary to this theory: Only three out of four mitered corners can be perfect on the same quilt on the first try!

Adding Borders the Blunt Corner Way

The crucial part of making blunt corners is always to add the sides of all borders on the same quilt in the same order. I almost always add the two side borders first, and then the top and bottom. (Look at the Dresden Plate or Ohio Star diagrams). I like the way that looks, plus it makes the side borders and end borders closer to the same length.

How to Piece Borders, Flaps, and Bindings

If you are going to piece borders, flaps, or bindings, place the pieces at right angles and stitch diagonally as if you were piecing bias strips (Figure 2). This eliminates bulk when the flaps and bindings are folded, and the seams appear less visible in a border.

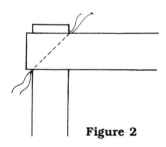

Figure 2

The What, Where, When, and How of Flaps

A flap is just that. In sewing terminology, it might be described as piping without the cord.

A flap is used when you need a tiny bit of color as an accent or to delineate. Just as an extra mat with a tiny edge of color may be the perfect thing when framing a picture, a flap can add the perfect touch to a quilt. It can go between borders or be used just before the binding, as in the Slate Blue Mosaic.

While the flap may look as if it is just tucked in between two layers of fabric when a seam is sewn, it isn't. It must be added separately, just like a border and in the same order as the borders, or the corners won't overlap correctly.

The most common width of flap that I use is ¼ inch. That means I cut a strip 1 inch wide on the straight grain, then fold and press it in half lengthwise. I then line the raw edges of the flap up with the raw edges of the last section of the quilt and stitch it in position. Then I proceed with the next border or binding. Yes, it does encroach ¼ inch onto the piece it is laid on, but I have never found that to be objectionable.

WHAT KIND OF BATTING?

What kind of quilting you are going to do, the end result desired, and where you live all help determine the kind of batting you will want. For minimal machine quilting, with a moderate amount of quilting, my favorite batting is bonded polyester in a medium weight sometimes called all-purpose. To me, one of the important characteristics to look for is bonding throughout, not just at the surface. And it must be soft. Some bonded batts have given a bad name to bonded batting because they become very stiff. Machine quilting is also stiffer than hand quilting, so you want to start with as soft a batt as possible. Bonding throughout is important to help eliminate fiber migration. (That's the term used to describe those little hairy fibers protruding through the quilt.)

There are typically three weights of batting available in the marketplace. They have different names, but, generally speaking, there is an average-weight batt used for most things. Generally, you want the all-purpose batting for machine quilting.

Low-loft is used by lots of hand quilters because it accepts small stitches more easily. Machine quilters who are going to do lots of quilting are also turning to low-loft batting. By hand or machine, when you don't want much puff, as with garments and place mats, you require low-loft batting or fleece. Most people feel low-loft does not add enough dimension to minimal machine quilting.

Thick batts are used when the end result you want is a comforter look. You might select that for tying, for example. If the batt is too thick, you may have to machine-quilt in sections and assemble as with the Quilt-As-You-Sew projects in Chapter 8.

Cotton battings and a cotton/polyester blend, available for several years, are regaining popularity as people spend more time and effort quilting by hand or machine. Generally, these batts must be more heavily quilted to prevent balling up when they are washed. But as cotton batting is being rediscovered, more and more companies create new cotton batting, so I would advise talking with a knowledgeable shop owner or quilter about the characteristics of particular cotton batts before selecting one.

Many battings are distributed on a regional, not national basis—because of freight costs—so to get really specialized batts, you may have to search out a mail-order quilting catalog. As of this writing, one company, Hobbs, offers a black quilt batt—really a smoky gray—that has been very well received for dark quilts.

PREPARING THE BACKING

Because I prefer a separate binding, my backings only need to be about 2 inches bigger in all directions than the quilt top. Even that is more for convenience than necessity. (If you want to bind the edges by bringing the backing around to the front, the backing needs to be larger. How much larger depends on how wide you want the finished binding to be.) On small crib or wall quilts it's usually not necessary to piece backings. The typical 45-inch-wide fabric is wide enough and you just cut it slightly longer than the quilt. Sixty, 90, and even 108-inch-wide fabrics are becoming more available to make unpieced backings for larger quilts. Some people try sheets for backings, but sheets are usually a tighter weave and most aren't 100 percent cotton. You might consider them an option for machine quilting, but they are definitely not recommended for hand quilting.

Usually a quilt back is made from one fabric, with minimal piecing. Nothing says that is the way it has to be. In fact, I find more and more of my quilt backs incorporating some degree of patchwork, a trick that allows me to use up fabric from my reserves so I can buy new fabric for tops!

Quilt Backings from One Fabric

The most common pieced back is a single seam centered lengthwise (Figure 1).

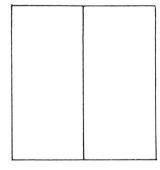

Figure 1

Sometimes it is advantageous to make cross-wise seams (Figure 2).

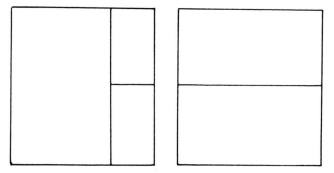

Figure 2

Scrap Quilt Backings

The quilt backs photographed give some idea of the fun you can have with scrap backs. The longer I make quilts, the harder it is for me to buy 6½ yards of a fabric I really love just to put on the back of a quilt. It is even harder, however, for me to buy 6½ yards of something I really don't like much but buy because it is a bargain.

It is especially easy to use scrap backings with quilts that are made by the block. Sometimes I back those squares with two alternating fabrics, making a checkerboard surface.

Remember, there is no more appropriate place to use a scrap backing than on a scrap quilt!

LAYERING A QUILT TOP

This method would be appropriate for tying, machine quilting, or hand quilting in a hoop. With most full-size quilt frames, the layering is done after putting the quilt in the frame, rather than before.

You will need:

- *At least one quilt top, batting, and backing for layering.* The backing should be pieced and pressed and the top pressed. It is easy to see at this point how directional pressing of seam allowances as you piece a quilt makes this step much easier. Check to make sure the quilt's opposite sides are the same length.
- *A table.* Not just any table. A relatively long narrow table is best. The necessary size of the table depends on the quilt size, but you need a table at least 5 feet long for a double or queen-size quilt. Wall hangings and crib quilts can be done on a

smaller table. Quilting does not work on a Ping-Pong table; it does not work on a carpeted floor, round table, or king-size bed. It's nice if your table has a center crack, but if it doesn't, just measure and mark the center of both ends.

The table you use must not be a priceless antique, or even a pretty good one, because there is too great a potential for scratching the table surface. You can put protective mats or cardboard cutting board on your table, but it will be better if you can find an alternate firm surface.

- *A friend.* You can layer a wall hanging or crib quilt alone, but for larger quilts, a friend makes layering easier and more fun. You *can* do it alone if you must.
- *Two yardsticks or tape measures.*
- *Safety pins.* The minimum number for a queen/double quilt is about 350 pins. A crib quilt will use at least 75 pins. I like chrome plated #1 pins (they're about ¾ inch long).

The Actual Layering Process

1. After everything is gathered, the object is to center all three layers in a "stack" on the table. Center the backing fabric on the table wrong side up. (Center it both lengthwise and crosswise.) Using a lengthwise center seam or marked center line in the backing fabric as a guide, line it up with the center of the table. Compare until you (and your friend) have the same number of inches hanging off each end.

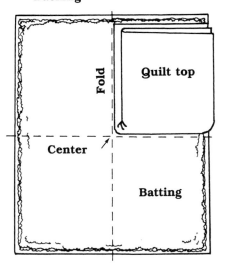

2. Add the layer of batting in the same way. Smooth it out carefully. (It's a good idea to remove packaged batting from the bag a day or two in advance, so it can relax. A careful steam press can eliminate difficult humps and bumps.) Make sure the batting completely covers the backing fabric.

3. Now fold the quilt top in half, right sides together, and lay the fold on the center line. Now carefully open the quilt top. Make sure equal lengths drop off the ends. (If you must work alone, mark the center of the table on the quilt batt, fold the quilt top in quarters, and place the double fold at the center point.) Open carefully.

4. Most quilt tops will be flat enough that you can just smooth them out. However, if you've had real problems piecing and the quilt top is very bumpy, you'll have to pat (in some cases pound) those bumps down. The fabric will scrunch up some in rough spots and you'll have to ease the top as you quilt, but it will look flat when you're through. If the bumps are really bad, you may have to shift to a fat batt. That will absorb the discrepancies better. The weight of the layers hanging off the table helps keep the fabrics smooth.

Start Pinning

How the quilt lies on the table, how it hangs, and how you pin it all determine the position of the three layers when you quilt.

1. Start in the middle and start pinning every 4 inches or in another selected pattern. Think about your quilting plan now, so that you avoid pinning where you will later want to stitch.

One of the real benefits of pinning rather than basting is that you don't put your hand under the quilt and move it out of position. Just pin from the top. When you feel the pin point touch the table top, pull it back up through the quilt and close. Basting is more disruptive and takes longer. Straight pins are not practical, because they catch on the quilt and can scratch you badly as you are working.

The number of pins per block or section depends on how many pins you have, how complicated the block is, and so on. I recommend starting with more than you think you need and using less when you are more experienced. Pin from the center out on the entire table surface.

2. Pull the quilt to one side so that a new center section is on the table and work to one end. Every

time you move the quilt, double-check to make sure you haven't developed wrinkles or folds in the backing fabric.

3. When you have completed that half, go back to the center and start in the other direction.

WHICH QUILTING TECHNIQUE WILL YOU USE?

Hand Quilting

Experiment with different methods until you find one you like. Don't forget to get a comfortable thimble. The quilting stitch is a small, consistent running stitch. There is a lot of discussion about the appropriate number of stitches per inch. The beginner should look for consistency first and strive for smaller stitches later.

- *In a full-size frame.* There are so many different frames, and each seems to be used slightly differently, so just follow the instructions for the one you own.
- *Hoops* to hold and floor stand hoops are also readily available.
- *Without a hoop or frame.* Some people prefer quilting without the tautness of the hoop or frame, especially if they are quilting by the block and then assembling the quilt.

Machine Quilting

Give serious consideration to machine quilting. I love hand quilting—both doing it and seeing it. Hand-quilting aficionados and anyone who has completely hand-quilted anything have a great appreciation for the hours of work. The uninitiated, however, almost invariably look at a hand-quilted quilt, then look up inquisitively and ask, "Did you do that by hand?" You beam "Yes" and then simply cannot believe the next question: "Couldn't they invent a machine to do all that?"

You can't, of course, use any machine to make a hand stitch, but you can use a sewing machine to quilt and get a real quilt. In the early years of the current quilting revival, machine quilting wouldn't have been considered acceptable, but people are more realistic today. Remember, everything's a trade-off. Piecing and quilting by hand, because they were once done that way and that is what you want to reproduce, are fine. Doing it all by hand in order to make it a "real quilt" is foolishness. Machine quilting is real. In fact, machine quilting may take more skill than hand quilting. It's a different skill. It is also much faster.

While I love hand quilting, I love making quilt tops more. I've learned there's little personal satisfaction in a pile of unquilted tops.

Many of the quilts in this book are perfect for straight line machine quilting and were finished that way. Their straight design lines are easy to follow with machine stitching. While hand quilting can enhance any quilt, I believe you should save hand quilting for areas where it will really show. When the overall graphic design can stand alone without your really missing hand quilting, you, like me, may decide you don't want to waste a lot of time and effort. Until you get within a few feet or sometimes inches of a quilt, what you see is not the stitching, but the shadow created by the quilting indentation. Machine quilting actually gives a crisper indentation.

Nearly everyone wonders if you need a fancy machine to do the quilting. I have successfully machine-quilted with all kinds of machines, from very simple to the most expensive. Check your machine's quilting I.Q. on scraps first. If you have any problem, or don't like the look of the stitch, the first thing to check is the pressure of the presser foot. Too much pressure can give an undesirable rippling effect. Nearly every machine has an even-feed attachment available that helps move all layers through the machine at the same rate. (Pfaff makes a wonderful machine with a built-in even-feed feature.) The second thing to do, especially when using invisible thread, is to check your tension. With invisible thread, you must relax the top tension. The thread is prone to stretching, and if the tension is too tight, it stretches as you stitch, then gathers up the fabric when it is cut.

Combine Hand and Machine Quilting

There are many opportunities for combining machine and hand quilting. Think about doing the long tedious seams and borders by machine either "in the ditch" or Quilt-As-You-Sew, and doing hand quilting in exposed blocks or borders where it will really show!

Tying

Tied quilts have yarn or heavy thread stitched through all layers and tied securely, usually in a square knot. The tying is usually done in a pattern, such as in the center of every square.

WHAT ABOUT THREAD?

For Machine Quilting

- *Invisible thread.* Actually, "transparent" is the word on most packages, but "invisible" sounds like more fun. It is a very fine nylon, not at all like the fishing line stuff used in the late 1960s. It comes in clear and smoky. The smoky thread looks very dark on the spool, but used one strand at a time, it's my favorite on everything but white and the lightest pastels. The clear thread reflects light on medium to dark fabrics.

  You will develop a real appreciation for invisible thread when you are quilting a high-contrast quilt. Let's say you are quilting "stitch in the ditch" style on a navy blue and white quilt, for example, and you have selected the navy thread. Any place you miss and where the thread stitches on the white fabric, your stitches will be visible from thirty feet away in the moonlight.
- *Regular sewing machine thread* for the bobbin should match the color of your backing fabric.

For Hand Quilting

- *Quilting thread.* In the past, most thread called "quilting thread" was intended for hand quilting only. Now there are some very nice threads labeled for either hand or machine quilting that I often use on the top of my sewing machine when not using invisible thread. But I still use the regular-weight cotton thread on my bobbin. The new quilting thread can also be used for hand quilting and comes in a wide range of colors, but it is not as heavy as the traditional hand-quilting thread.

WHEN THE QUILT IS LAYERED

If you are tying, now is the time. If hand-quilting, arrange your hoop in the center of the quilt and carefully quilt from the center out. The most questions arise if you want to machine-quilt.

When you finish pinning, you are going to look at that quilt and say, "The part I still don't understand is how to get that great big quilt through the little opening in my sewing machine." That's right, the question is, how do you stay in control of the quilt? The answer is, by making it smaller and more manageable.

The first seam to quilt is the longest center seam. Everything to the right of that seam as you sit at the sewing machine must go through the arch. Starting at the edge, roll that side up to within 4 or 5 inches of the seam. To the left of the seam, fold the quilt in 9 or 10-inch folds to the same distance from the seam (Figure 1).

Now it's a long thin quilt. Starting at the end opposite where you will start sewing, roll the quilt up like a sleeping bag. Suddenly you have a manageable quilt (Figure 2). Carry it to the machine.

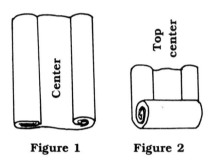

Figure 1   **Figure 2**

Setting Up the Machine

Invisible nylon thread goes on the top only. Matching thread is okay on the top if low- or no-contrast fabrics are used.

While I like to use ten to twelve stitches per inch for machine piecing, I change the stitch length to eight to ten stitches per inch for quilting.

Machine Quilting "in the Ditch"

"In the ditch" refers to stitching in the space created between two pieces of fabric that are sewn together. "What space?" you may ask. Granted there isn't much, so you create a little more space by applying slight tension. Use your fingers to pull fabric away from the seam as the sewing machine feed dog pulls the fabric through the machine. That slight tension creates the extra space for stitching. When your fingers release the tension, the fabric returns to its natural position and hides the stitching "in the ditch."

Start Quilting

1. Sit at the machine with the rolled quilt in your lap. Position the quilt so that the end of the seam you are quilting is under the needle. Lower the presser foot and start quilting. With both hands, pull away from the seam to make the ditch. You'll discover forgotten muscles in your shoulders. Stop and relax your back and shoulders between rows. Keep the quilt loose enough so that its weight doesn't pull against the needle.

If a friend is helping you, you have a catcher. If not, you'll probably want a table in front of your sewing machine so the quilted section won't fall to the floor and pull.

2. When you have finished that seam, the next one to quilt is the longest seam perpendicular to the seam just finished, usually the center horizontal seam. I hate to be the one to have to tell you, but you have to reroll for every seam. Machine quilting goes in fast, but it isn't fast to take out. You must stay in control of the quilt. As you reroll, check the quilt back for newly sewn pleats. It's a personal decision, but I don't take out the little puckers often found at seam crossings. If there's a tuck you could catch your toe in, you will have to correct it. Smaller tucks in between are a personal judgment call.

3. When you are all done, check the back again and check the front; trim any missed threads. (I like to trim threads as I go, so they don't get caught in other rows of stitching.) Remove the pins and get ready to add the borders or binding.

Other Kinds of Machine Quilting

You can also machine-quilt on the surface of the fabric instead of in the ditch. The main difference is that you have to mark a design or work out a plan for the quilting.

Free-form quilting adds another direction. While straight line quilting on the machine is really quite simple, free-form takes a little more practice. You disengage, or lower, the feed dogs. The needle still goes up and down, but the machine no longer moves the fabric. That means you become the power moving the quilt, and you can move it any direction you want.

ADDING BORDERS QUILT-AS-YOU-SEW

This method of finishing is appropriate for any quilt where the interior section is already quilted, whether traditionally or by the block or sections. Many of the quilts shown in this book are finished this way. It happens that they were all machine-quilted, but the technique could also be used with a hand-quilted interior section. One of the main advantages is how much smaller the interior of the quilt is without the borders, and how much easier it is to manipulate during the quilting process.

Very few people have considered that in an 84 by 100-inch quilt with 10-inch borders, the borders make up 38 percent of the surface area. If you can economize on effort without sacrificing effect, this method for adding borders is very worthwhile. The best thing about Quilt-As-You-Sew is that you are making a seam to add a border no matter what, so why not quilt at the same time?

Determining Sizes for All Border Pieces

Determining the Widths

1. Assuming you will use multiple borders, determine the finished size of each and their total width. For example, on the World Without End Quilt, the borders are 3, 2, and 5 inches each from the inside out. That is a total border width of 10 inches. Confirm that the borders you have settled on will create the desired final-size quilt.

2. Add 1 inch to the total border width for the width of the batting. Add the same amount for the width of the border backing fabric if you are planning a separate binding. If, instead, you plan to bring the backing fabric around to the front to bind the edge, you will need to add at least 1¾ to 2 inches to the border width for the border backing width.

3. Add ½ inch to the width of each border measurement to allow for seam allowances.

To Figure the Length of the Pieces

1. Measure the quilted interior section of the quilt. In the World Without End example, that was 60 inches by 80 inches.

2. The side borders are sewn on first. The length of the quilt and the length of all the side borders will be the same. You may add an inch or two for slight discrepancies, but if more than that gets eased into a seam—because of bad tension, for example—the border will start to ruffle.

3. The length of the first borders that go across the top and bottom of the quilt are equal to the measured quilt width, plus two times the width of the border itself, plus two ¼-inch seam allowances. For example, the border backing for the top and bottom of the World Without End Quilt was 80 inches long, the batting was 80 inches long, and the first border would have been 66½ inches long if it hadn't been a stripe. (See "Can You Miter Quilt-As-You-Sew Borders?" page 142.)

Adding the Borders

Adding the first border is the trickiest because it includes adding the border backing pieces and border batting.

1. Cut all four backing and batting strips and the first border the calculated size.

2. Lay the quilt on a large flat surface, right side up. Put the first border right side down on the quilt with the raw edges lined up on the long edge of the quilt. Pin sparingly. Fold the edge you are working on forward about 15 inches so that the border backing strip can be placed flat on the back of the quilt, right sides together, long edges aligned. Now lay the border batting on top of the backing. Line up long edges and ends. Pin securely in place through all six layers—that is, the border, three layers in the quilt, the border backing, and border batting (see Figure 1 and the Figure 1 cross-section).

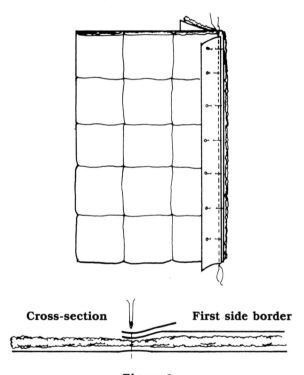

Cross-section　　　**First side border**

Figure 1

3. Machine-stitch ¼ inch from the edge through all layers, for the entire length of the quilt. At this point everything in the quilt is to the left of your sewing machine needle. Remove all pins. Trim away any excess batting in the seam to reduce bulk, but do not trim closer than ⅛ inch, or batting may pull out of the seam.

4. Pull all border sections away from the quilt and bring them together so they are flat on the same surface as the quilt. You will probably want to press this seam, even with steam.

5. Repeat on the opposite side of the quilt (Figure 2). When both borders are finished, trim all four ends so that they are straight with the quilt for the next seams.

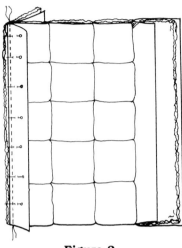

Figure 2

6. Add the end borders the same way. The only difference is that the first border must go from one outside edge of the already attached first border to the other outside edge. The border backing and border batting pieces should also extend to the extremities of their matching materials (Figure 3). Pin, stitch, trim, open and press in place as before.

Repeat on the final edges (Figure 4). When all four edges have been completed, the flat quilt will measure slightly larger than your calculated finished size; the first border will be securely in place, and the quilt will be ready for the second border to be added.

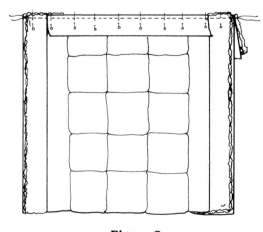

Figure 3

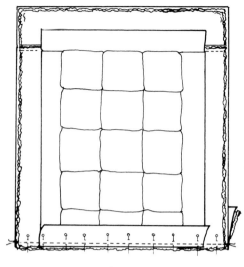

Figure 4

Adding the Additional Borders

1. Measure the exact length of the first border. Cut two pieces of the second border that long and the desired width. (Don't forget the seam allowances.) The second border is added very much like the stitch-and-flip process described in Chapter 5, "String Quilting." Carefully smooth the first border and pin it in place sparingly.

2. Starting with the long edges, place the second border on top of the first, right sides touching and raw edges aligned (Figure 5). Pin in place and

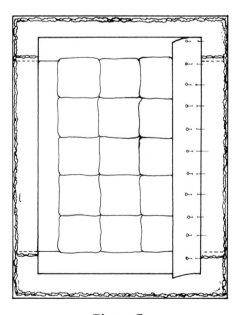

Figure 5

stitch, this time through only four layers: border backing, border batting, first border, and second border. As you sew there will be a narrow width of batting and backing to the right of your needle and all the rest of the quilt will be to the left of the needle. Remove the pins, and open the second border so that its wrong side is against the batting. Smooth and/or press lightly into place. Repeat on the opposite side of the quilt.

3. The length of the end borders is the same as the measurement from the outside edge of the quilt border to the outside edge of the border on the opposite side of the quilt. Cut pieces and proceed.

4. You can add as many borders as you like this way. For the most pleasing corners, always add borders to a quilt in the same sequence—both sides first and then the ends.

Can You Miter Quilt-As-You-Sew Borders?

Mitering the first border on a Quilt-As-You-Sew finish is the most difficult. Because the first border on the World Without End Quilt was a stripe, we felt compelled to miter the corners and now I feel compelled to tell you how to do it.

1. As with any mitered corner, the borders must be cut longer. Double the width of the first border and add that to the calculated length, then add a few more inches so that you don't have to center the border perfectly.

2. The only difference in the seaming results from the necessity to leave the striped border free at the corner seams. On the first seams (through all six layers), stop stitching about ⅜ inch from the end of the quilt on all four corners, and backstitch. Remove all pins and pull the border out of the seam line. Take a few stitches by hand to hold the remaining five layers together until the next seam crosses.

When you start across the end seams through all six layers, once again, pull the ends of the border out of the seam line, stitch from the edge to the first intersection, stop ¼ inch from the corner, start again on the other side of the border edge. Stop and start in this way at all four border intersections.

When the fabric is pulled flat onto the border batting, fold one ragged end flat and one at a 45-degree angle and hand-stitch them in place.

MAKING THE BINDING

French Fold Binding

Most of my bindings are cut on the straight, preferably unseamed lengthwise grain and folded in half. My favorite width for binding is whatever I think will look best on a particular quilt. Some quilts look best with the tiniest ⅜-inch finished binding. Others need a ¾ to 1-inch binding. Look at our quilt pictures to see how varied the decisions have been.

My favorite binding is cut four times the desired finished width *plus* ½ inch for two seam allowances *and* ⅛ inch to ¼ inch to go around the edge of the quilt. The fatter the batt, the more you need to allow here. Fold and press in half so that the raw edges are touching.

Usually I stitch all the way around the quilt, ¼ inch from the raw edge of the patchwork, and then trim away excess quilt batting and backing. Because I like full-feeling bindings, I cut batting and backing almost, but not quite, twice as wide as the desired finished binding.

Lay the binding on your quilt so that both raw edges of the binding match the raw edge of the quilt top, and stitch in place (Figure 1). When the binding is stitched onto the quilt and pulled flat onto the batting, it should be about ¼ inch wider than the batting (Figure 2).

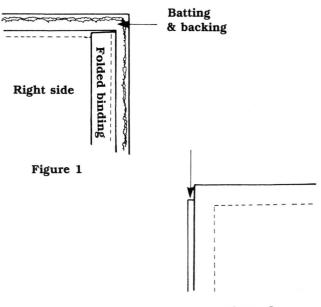

Batting & backing

Right side

Folded binding

Figure 1

Figure 2

Roll binding around the raw edge of quilt to the back, and hand-stitch in place using the row of machine stitching as a stabilizer and a guide. Add binding strips in the same order as with the borders.

To make blunt corners, add bindings on the sides of the quilt first, and complete the hand stitching. Measure the quilt ends carefully. Add ½ inch at each binding end. To eliminate raw edges, turn that back on the wrong side before stitching in place.

The hand hemming stitch I use is hidden. The needle comes out of the quilt, takes a bite of the binding, and re-enters the quilt exactly behind the stitch. The thread is carried in the layers of quilt, not on the outside. At corners, carefully stitch ends shut (Figure 3).

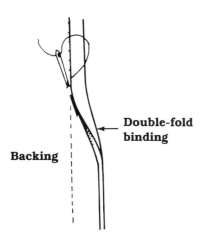

Backing

Double-fold binding

Figure 3

If you are hemming the binding by machine, attach binding to the back and bring to the front and either top-stitch with invisible thread or experiment with your machine hemming stitch.

Bias Bindings

Bias is only necessary if the edge is curvy. Some people believe that bias will wear longer, but I have no evidence to show that it does or that extra wear would outweigh the extra time and trouble to make bias bindings. The fact that bias bindings typically ripple more when applied to a straight-edge quilt is most important to me.

You can do French fold bias bindings. The instructions are the same as above, except the bindings are cut on the bias instead of straight grain. That is what we used on the Mini-Spools Quilt.

IT'S NOT DONE UNTIL IT'S SIGNED

Current quilt historians are handicapped by anonymous ancestral quilters. No one knows which quilts will be examined for clues a hundred years from now. So help stamp out anonymity. Sign your quilt. This can be done simply or in elaborate detail. It can go on the front or the back and be subtle or shout. Cross stitch or embroidery are lovely if you like to do them. A simple way is to use an indelible marking pen or laundry pen to write your name, date, and any inscription on a piece of prewashed muslin. Then hand-stitch this to the back of the quilt.

Index

Note: Entries given in italics indicate projects featured in this book.

All of us at Meredith® Press are dedicated to offering you, our customer, the best books we can create. We are particularly concerned that all of the instructions for making projects are clear and accurate. Please address your correspondence to: Customer Service Department, Meredith® Press, Meredith Corporation, 150 East 52nd Street, New York, NY 10022.

Scrap Patchwork & Quilting is the fifth in a series of quilting books. If you would like the first four books in the series, Country Patchwork & Quilting 1988, Romantic Patchwork & Quilting 1989, Classic Patchwork & Quilting 1990, and Seasonal Patchwork & Quilting 1991, please write to Better Homes and Gardens Books, P.O. Box 10670, Des Moines, IA 50336, or call 1-800-678-2665.